Endorsements f

"If there is a 'required reading list for new parents, employed parents with questions about their values, or employers who are concerned about the family life of their needed employees—this book should be on that list!

The author has done her homework through personal experience, through the research and survey responses of a wide variety of people at many different stages of home, family and employment life.

The experiences, insights and stories of many parents and children will provide the reader with multiple stimulations and resources for evaluating their quality and quantity of parenting, reducing or increasing work hours, budgeting, prioritizing, self-care, etc. This is a book worth investing in! It will pay dividends for a lifetime!"

–Rev. Dr. David S. Belasic, Pastor and past president of the Eastern Lutheran District and father of three

"It was our plan to be able to have one of us at home to raise our children. There are many ideas and suggestions in this book that made it easier for us to accomplish this goal. As a father, it is a good feeling to know that my wife is able to be at home with our children as much as possible."

–Dr. Michael Fabrizzi, Physical Therapist and Athletic Trainer and father of two

"Tough financial times are going to make the 'luxury' of living on one salary even tougher for young couples with children. Cathi's well-researched and parent-tested advice about how to make lifestyle changes in order to spend more time at home with your children is more valuable now than ever. From making that initial decision to increase the quality of your family life through creating an action plan, Cathi's got it covered. And so can YOU!"

–Mary Lou Kish, M.S., Assistant Professor and mother of four

"Deciding to work from home can be a scary proposition. While cutting back or losing a salary can seem devastating, it doesn't have to be. Ms. Doebler offers insight and alternatives for the working family. By using her experience and knowledge, Ms. Doebler allows families to refocus, gain perspective, and decide whether working from home is the right option for them."

–Erin Coss, k2e books, Inc., co-author of *My Hospital Journal*, and mother of three

"This book is very timely! In a time when both parents work to have the things they want, this book really focuses on the value of being a parent and raising children in today's world. The author has shown that you can have the best of both worlds without sacrificing the needs of the child. The blessings that will come from reading the book and then determining a plan for your life will cause a lasting reward."

–William D. Cochran, Director of School Ministry, District and Congregational Services, Lutheran Church Missouri Synod

"As a mother of two, who gave up her career to be home with her children, I can see how this book would provide a wealth of information for families looking for ways to simplify and prioritize in order to put the needs of their children first. No one is going to raise your children like you will, so if you are looking for concrete advice on how to cut costs to live on one income or on how to lighten your work load—this book is for you! Cathi speaks from personal experience and has also spent hours doing research and gathering surveys from others who have been successful in putting their family first."

–Michele Thiele, certified teacher and mother of two

"While working with expectant mothers, I often hear about the ways they are trying to provide balance for their families. This book addresses many of the challenges that these new mothers face, and provides solid and useful ideas for those challenges."

–John M. Budzinski, M.D.

Ditch the Joneses

DISCOVER YOUR FAMILY

How to Thrive on Less Than Two Incomes!

CATHI BRESE DOEBLER

Ditch the Joneses; Discover Your Family by Cathi Brese Doebler

Author's photo by Paul Gerlach

COVER, INTERIOR DESIGN & PRINT PRODUCTION:
Eastco Multi Media Solutions, Inc.
3646 California Rd.
Orchard Park, NY 14127
www.eastcomultimedia.com

Designer: Heather Huether

Printed in Canada

This book is dedicated to:
my husband, who supported me through it all;
my boys, who are the reason this book was born; and
my mom, who made having a part-time business possible.

Thank you to:
the parents who inspired me with their creativity
and devotion to their children;
Holt Vaughn and his team at Vaughnstreet.com for their guidance;
my editors Sandra Rice, Sharon Fabrizzi, and Sue Brese;
and to the Lord for His guidance through parenthood.

Contents

Introduction

"I just wish I could stay home with my kids," she told me, "but we really can't afford to lose my salary." Her eyes glistened with tears, and my heart ached for her. She wanted so desperately to be home with her children every day and was not able to make that choice.

There are many parents who don't feel they have the choice between working and staying at home, and many of those parents struggle with so many emotions as they wave good-bye to their little ones when they leave for work every morning. For some, it is a daily occurrence, and they feel helpless. My prayer for you is that this book can help you focus and determine whether you can do something you never thought possible…spend more time at home.

This book is for parents who:

- Desire to reduce their hours to part-time
- Desire to stay home full-time
- Desire to explore new ideas with time and financial management
- Desire to consider options while deciding on their family's lifestyle

Since the time I could talk, my family referred to me as the one who asks questions. Most thought I'd become a reporter because I tended to "get the scoop" out of every relative and visitor, without interrupting. People generally just kept talking. So, naturally, working in human resources, I was able to talk and share with many mothers. And I started to notice many similar comments. Comments of struggles between finances and time at home with their children. Comments of guilt, frustration, and sadness over missing their child's first steps, daily lunchtime discoveries, and cuddles following afternoon naps. I heard parents agonizing over their difficult decisions and was fortunate enough to hear these comments before I had children.

So when the time came for my husband and me to join the world of parenthood, we had been forewarned and advised by those who had gone before us, and having listened carefully, we were able to make some solid decisions for our own family.

By planning before our first child arrived, praying to the Lord for guidance, and making changes to our lifestyle, we were blessed to be able to live on one salary. After our first child was born, I began researching this topic even more. I realized that those same parents who had commented about their struggles were still "out there." And those parents had younger siblings, friends, and other family members who might be going through the same struggle. Why not share what my husband and I had learned with those people?

I realized also that there were other parents who had creatively made a way for their families to survive on one income or one and a half incomes. As a result, these parents had a lot they could share also. So my research moved toward those men and women—I conducted a survey for parents who had reduced or eliminated their work hours in order to be home more with their kids.

I was very excited by the response to the survey. I received completed surveys from men and women all over the United States, and even one from Europe. Their surveys were full of fantastic ideas to help parents with financial savings and with the emotional changes that come from being new parents. I am thankful to these parents who shared their "war stories." They are truly the heroes of this book.

Based on my own experience, research, and the surveys, I designed and began teaching a class to other parents on how they could try to be home with their families more. The class had the following purposes:

- To discuss family balance as a priority
- To share research based on others who have reduced work hours, and their advice
- To give participants ideas on how to financially prepare for and adjust to a smaller income, continue to have adult relationships and interactions if they leave work or reduce their work hours, and adjust through the transition period from working full-time hours to part-time or no hours

After teaching this class, it made sense to enhance the same basic points and share them with more parents through a book. I couldn't possibly travel the country to teach this class when the whole point was to be home with my children. And so this book was born.

You may disagree with some of the material provided in this book. I know that some of the opinions shared may not be what you want to hear. I also realize that some of the opinions shared may not be what you have believed in the past. But after reading this, you may want to make changes in your life to help your family come first.

I hope you enjoy the journey! The next section is a devotion written by my sister, Sandra Brese Rice, to help you begin your journey.

A Devotional Thought to Begin Your Journey

> At that time the disciples came to Jesus, saying, "Who then is greatest in the kingdom of heaven?" And He called a child to Himself and set him before them, and said, "Truly I say to you, unless you are converted and become like children, you will not enter the kingdom of heaven. *Whoever then humbles himself as this child, he is the greatest in the kingdom of heaven.* And whoever receives one such child in My name receives Me."
>
> —Matthew 18:1-5, NAS, emphasis added

Congratulations! If you are picking up this book, you must be beginning a new family adventure! How exciting, and yet, how scary…after all, your family structure and schedules will now inevitably change with either new babies or a different income.

"Whoever then humbles himself as this child, he is the greatest in the kingdom of heaven." Humility…Webster says humility can be defined as *the quality of being without pride*. It also defines pride as *excessive self-esteem*. Whoa! This is tough in today's world! People are honored for their wealth and place in society. They are given awards for success in the workplace and are given raises based on overtime. Many feel their *self-worth* is judged by their paycheck and status—Christ, however, does not.

It is hard to be a parent. You will face challenges…but you are not alone!

My six-year-old son came home from school one day with a journal entry in hand. He was so excited to show me that he had actually written a story all by himself! "Look, Mommy!" he said. "I can write now with no help from anybody!" I looked down at the page and smiled. The tears began to form…he had two stick-like figures on the page with the "words" written…*I feel better when my mom hugs me.*

What more could you ask for?

It is hard to be a parent. You will face challenges…but you are not alone!

Zachary and I could spend hours in the store…not buying, just looking. The unique thing is that he doesn't covet; he just explores. This, of course, drives my husband and daughter crazy! They are the "get in and get out" types. Zach and I, well, we linger, doddle, and enjoy the moment. On one such occasion, however, he and I actually did have a plan. It was Daddy's birthday, and he wanted to get the "most specialist" gift ever.

After walking the entire mall, I looked down at Zach and noticed that he had tears in his eyes. "Don't worry, Zach," I said. "We'll find him a gift; it will be all right."

"It's not that, Mom," he said. "It's just that, well, it is so great to get to be with you today."

What more could you ask for?

It is hard to be a parent. You will face challenges...but you are not alone!

Emma, at age three, during a morning snuggle, said, "Mama, you're my best friend...I just love your face." What more could you ask for?

It is hard to be a parent. You will face challenges...but you are not alone!

My daughter is my little missionary. She has a strong childlike faith that she shares with everyone. One day we were listening to a book on tape in the car, and Eeyore's gloomy comment was, "Who knows..." From the back seat of the mini-van, Emma yelled, "God knows!"

Her brother replied, "Sorry, Emma, God isn't in this story."

And Emma said, "Well, He should be because He knows everything! They should just ask Him!"

What more could you ask for?

It is hard to be a parent. You will face challenges...but you are not alone!

Throughout the Bible, many people gave up worldly possessions or worldly status to do what they felt was right. Noah lived with years of ridicule from his neighbors as he built the ark. How lonely and crazy this may have seemed at times for him...but he was never alone. Genesis 8:1 says, "But God remembered Noah..." (NIV).

Moses lived in the palace and was raised as a prince, yet he led the Israelites to the Promised Land as a shepherd. All the while, God was telling him that he would not be alone. Exodus 3:12 says, "And God said, 'I will be with you...'" (NIV).

The Lord told Joshua, "...Be strong and courageous. Do not be terrified; do not be discouraged, for the LORD your God will be with you wherever you go" (Joshua 1:9, NIV).

He will be with you as well as you struggle to decide a direction for your family and as you look for opportunities to spend less on possessions and more on quality time with your family. He will be with you when you feel discouraged. He will be with you when your feelings are hurt by others or when you feel worthless by today's standards. He will be with you through your joys and tears, your laughter and fears. Let Him in...He WILL be with you...you are not alone!

What more could you ask for?

Dear Lord,

Watch over us today as we begin a new journey with our family. Help us to see the path that You want our family to follow. Help us to accept the best direction and decision that You see for us, with the faith and understanding that You know best and that You will always be with us...guiding us and supporting us along the way. Help us to have patience, Lord, patience for this process and with each other. Thank You for loving us and for giving us Your Word, the Bible, so that we may see examples of Your love for Your people.

Amen.

—Sandra Brese Rice (© 2010)
Contributor to Chicken Soup for the Soul
Devotional Stories for Women

Part 1

DISCOVERING YOUR DIRECTION

CHAPTER 1

Why Did You Pick This Book Off the Shelf?

Your kids are only little once, and if you can afford to stay home part or all of the time, you'll never regret it.

—A Stay-at-Home Mom

I once heard my son, who was four at the time, tell his grandfather, "Grandpa, a long time ago when I was three..." I couldn't help but laugh. To a four-year-old, one year was practically a lifetime, one-fourth of his life, actually. Comments like that, however, help me to understand the struggle of waiting for Christmas or sometimes even something as simple as the phrase "after dinner." For adults, time flies by quickly, and in a wink, those four years have come and gone. How blessed I have been to witness every day and participate in each of my sons' milestones. I am so thankful for those precious years and so excited about what is to come. I hope that you are interested in this book because you want to experience the same.

You Are Not Alone

In a poll by Survey USA, 73 percent of moms surveyed said being a two-income family doesn't allow enough time with the kids, and 87 percent said they would prefer to be home if they could afford to.[1]

Raising children who have been loaned to us for a brief moment outranks every other responsibility. Besides, living by that priority when kids are small will produce the greatest rewards at maturity.[2]

When I taught classes on this topic, I asked the participants why they came to the training session. They had different answers but typically the same overall goal:

> What if I CAN make this work? What if we really could survive on one income? What if I could be home when my kids are little, when they are sick, when they are taking their first steps? What if I could be there when they leave for the school bus and when they come home again?

Don't Shut Down Yet!

As you begin to look at the suggestions made in this book, take time to consider why you are reading this. Knowing your purpose will help you to be open to the ideas that follow.

You Can't Do It Alone

Throughout this book there will be prayers, like the one below, that connect the ideas of each section with a related prayer to God:

Dear Lord,

Please open my heart as I read this book. Help me to make the right decisions for my family. Take away my fear, and help me to feel Your presence, knowing that You are with me through life's many challenges.

Amen.

CHAPTER 2

Financial Decisions Are Hard; You Are Not Alone!

> I'm richer now than I ever was, even though our income is half! Our son brings so much fulfillment to our lives. I am so glad that we've made sacrifices so that I can be here every day for him. We've never been so happy. Your kids are only young for a limited amount of time. Seize the opportunity to spend this precious time with them. It's definitely not easy making sacrifices, but the smiles, laughter, all of the "firsts" that YOU get to experience make any size paycheck seem immaterial.
>
> —Part-Time Job Developer

The economy has been frightening for so many people in the last year or two. Every day we hear depressing headlines about the value of the dollar decreasing, the cost of fuel increasing, and the high unemployment rates. In times like these we need to stretch ourselves more than we did when times were easier. Making smart decisions in our spending is something that we need to apply more often. Costs for groceries and gasoline are rising, and yet many companies are choosing to hold back annual raises in order to stay healthy or even just stay in business. The average family now has the same or less income than before, while paying more for necessary items like food. It can make us yearn for the past.

We've all heard one of our elders describe the past in this way, "Things were simpler then." Maybe you have even thought that when you've looked back on your own childhood experiences.

Regarding finances, this statement is true and yet untrue. Fifty years ago there were still families that struggled to survive on one income. The main difference then was that a one-income family was the norm. Today costs are skyrocketing, in some cases requiring two incomes for survival and in many cases pressuring parents to both work so that they can "keep up with the Joneses." Our culture can be incredibly materialistic and has a sad disregard for the precious time families need for each other. I wonder if many feel the way to be a good provider and parent is to keep up with the Joneses. Maybe some parents need to hear that it is OK to not provide everything material and to focus on time and spiritual upbringing for their children.

> America's materialistic value system runs very deep within the culture.... Today, when the culture is in a tug-of-war with families for control of our children, we can't afford to be casual about their care and training....There should be a way to avoid living in a state of perpetual chaos. It is hard on adults but it creates havoc for children.[1]

When I teach the classes on this topic, I ask participants to consider these questions:

1. How often do I let society tell me what to believe?
   ___ Never
   ___ Seldom
   ___ Sometimes
   ___ Always

2. How often do I question what the media tells me?
   ___ Never
   ___ Seldom
   ___ Sometimes
   ___ Always

3. How often do I listen to my heart and use my intuition to make my decisions for my family?
   ___ Never
   ___ Seldom
   ___ Sometimes
   ___ Always

4. How do we feel about two incomes or one income?

5. What do we feel that our family really needs?

6. Have we looked at prices of day care, formula, mileage to work, etc.?

7. Is owning a house a need, or is renting OK?

8. Is having two vehicles important for us?

9. Do we need to take large vacations?

10. What kind of education do we want for our children (i.e., public, private, etc.)?

11. Do we know how much private education costs?

12. Is cable a need for our family?

13. What is our definition of a "full life"?

14. Other thoughts I have on this issue include:

The point behind this exercise is to give parents time to reflect on how the culture that they have to deal with every day is leaving imprints on their decision making. How often are we making choices for our families based on what the culture is pushing as opposed to the true needs of our spouse and children? Do we as parents ever feel pressure to keep up rather than to slow down? Do we realize that time is flying by and that thinking through decisions such as who will spend daily time with our children are more important than ever?

This exercise can help us begin to take a look at assumptions we face in our everyday decision making. Before continuing on, take time to answer the fourteen questions above, recording your answers on the page or in a journal.

After completing this exercise, you are in a better position to consider God's plan for you and your family. Keeping His plan in mind will help you make better decisions.

> Since, then, you have been raised with Christ, set your hearts on things above, where Christ is seated at the right hand of God. Set your minds on things above, not on earthly things. For you died, and your life is now hidden with Christ in God. When Christ, who is your life, appears, then you also will appear with him in glory.
>
> —COLOSSIANS 3:1-4, NIV

When we listen to God's Word and live a life that honors Him, He is there as a constant, a rock to hold on to in hard times, a pillow to comfort us in sad times, and a song for us to sing in joyous times. Keeping God in the equation will help you live a life of fullness.

Some people might interpret the words "full life" to mean "having money," but money may not be the answer to a complete life. A full life may include financial stability, but it expands beyond finances; it includes our relationships with those we love and with God.

> But those who want to get rich fall into temptation and a snare and many foolish and harmful desires which plunge men into ruin and destruction. For the love of money is a root of all sorts of evil, and some by longing for it have wandered away from the faith, and pierced themselves with many griefs.
>
> —1 TIMOTHY 6:9-10, NAS

Having a lot of money won't give you a life without problems. "He who loves money will not be satisfied with money, nor he who loves abundance with its income" (Ecclesiastes 5:10, NAS).

If you struggle with a desire for more money or possessions than you need, ask the Lord for help in focusing your heart. "Jesus said, 'Let the children alone, and do not hinder them from coming to Me; for the kingdom of heaven belongs to such as these'" (Matthew 19:14, NAS). If Jesus places such an emphasis on children, it makes sense that He would get great pleasure from helping you love your family.

Jesus,

I am so thankful for Your love of children and Your love for my family. Help us to remember to look to You when we make decisions for our family. Help us to "keep You in the equation." The love of money is so tempting for us, and it is so easy to want more. Put Your arms of protection around our family, and steer our decision making so that our lives are truly full of Your presence. Amen.

Part 2

GETTING IT DONE

CHAPTER 3

Plan *Before* You Start a Family

Really learn more about yourself and what both "success" and "fulfillment" mean to you. Before leaving the workforce, practice living on less income.

—Human Resources Consultant

Your family is your responsibility, so planning for their future is critical.

Buying a Home

When my husband and I applied for a loan to buy our first home, we did not have children yet. The bank manager came into the office and handed my husband a piece of paper with some figures on it. "This is how much of a loan you can apply for," he said. I leaned over my husband's arm, looked at the number, and then looked up at him in surprise. The bank was prepared to give us a loan for which monthly payments would require *both* of our salaries in good-paying full-time jobs.

When we bought our house, however, we went with a much lower loan. We bought a house that we could afford on one salary...it was our first smart decision that was geared toward planning for our children.

Having the house of your dreams doesn't have to happen the first time around, especially when your children are small. In fact, people can happily survive on much less than they realize. How often have I heard people say that they couldn't possibly lose one of their two incomes because of their house payments alone? If you can't afford it on one income, don't buy it. Better yet, build up a cash fund for a few years while the kids are little, and then when you have a substantial down payment, buy your home.

If you haven't already bought a home or condo, but you plan to do so soon, remember that you need to consider the long-term impact of your purchase. Can you afford the home you want on only one salary? If not, why are you even considering it? Be smart about it. Think your finances through with a long-term plan in mind. Further on in this book are worksheets that will help you begin to do this.

If you are not in the market to buy a home and you decide to continue to rent an apartment, you may want to "shop around" to see if you can find a better deal. The price of apartments can range from cheap to ridiculously expensive. Pick a place that is affordable on one of your salaries.

Do a "Test Run"

If you plan before you have children, you can test your ability to live on one salary before one of you actually leaves your job. There are several ways to do this.

Savings are not overrated.

Put away some money in a savings account for emergencies. Ideally, you should have this money in savings before your first child arrives. This money should not be touched unless you have an emergency. This money should be enough for your family to survive for six months without either of your salaries. Remember that the amount you need will increase each time you add a new child to your family.

Practice makes perfect.

Try living for at least three months in a row on only one salary. This will give you time to see if you can do it and to see where and how you struggle in the process. You'll begin to discover which purchases you might have to give up and which spending habits you will need to change. During this three-month period, you can place the money you are not spending into a savings account.

Log your results.

For three months, keep a spending diary of all expenditures, even for small items like coffee. Pay attention not only to your predictable spending (i.e., school loan payments, house payments, car payments, etc.) but also to your unpredictable spending (i.e., coffee and doughnut breaks, expensive brand foods, dinners out, movie nights, etc.). By paying close attention to your spending, you will be able to look back and consider how you can make changes to your spending.

Plan Your Budget Each Year

Each year you should plan your annual family budget and then set monthly budgets together. By doing this with your spouse, you can make sure that you are "on the same page" regarding your finances. By looking ahead, you'll be better prepared for what is coming, and you'll be able to better plan for months that may drain your finances more than others. Spend time identifying your financial priorities, which will help you make fewer impulse buys and focus on what is truly a "need" as opposed to a "want." For example, when choosing a vehicle, if you are planning for a family you'll want to think about car seats and safety rather than about how sporty the vehicle is.

You will find a section called "Determining Your Budget" that you can use to look at your annual finances further along in this book.

Pay Off Credit Card Debt and Other Debts as Much as Possible

Credit card debt is one of the worst ways to lose control of your finances. Interest rates can be very cumbersome, and if you don't pay off the money you owe each month, you will pay much more in the end than you originally spent. If you have any credit card debts, try to pay them off before you add the costs of children to your budget.

Get out of debt as much as possible; get expert financial assistance if necessary. There will be some debt that you won't be able to just "pay off" quickly, like a house, but there may be other debt that you should try to pay off as soon as possible.

Live Within Your Means

Living within your means is basically a way of "using your common sense financially." If you can't afford it, don't buy it. End of story. If you don't *need* it but simply *want* it, don't buy it. How often do you make a purchase that is not truly something your family needs to survive? We have become so accustomed to having things in our culture that we often just make purchases without even considering if we really need it. For example, do you *need* to buy the name-brand foods, toys, and clothes? No. You *need* to buy food, but it could be a generic brand. Before you hand over your cash, think twice about your purchases. Be sure it is truly something that you need.

In his book *Smart Women Finish Rich*, David Bach gives many suggestions for controlling your spending. One suggestion that can really help is to start paying cash for things that you buy. The idea behind this is that when you pay for something with a credit card, you don't feel the significance at that moment of the amount you are spending. "Cash makes you think more about exactly how much you are spending and for what," wrote Bach. "You'd be surprised what a dramatic change this single action can make."[1]

Bach also suggests cutting up one of your credit cards. "The feeling of power you will get from this small token gesture can be tremendous," wrote Bach. "Remember, if worse comes to worse, you can always call the credit card company and order a new one."[2] A friend of mine took a similar approach when she put her credit cards in the freezer and literally "froze" them so she could not use them.

"Never spend more than $100 on anything without taking forty-eight hours to think about it," wrote Bach.[3] I agree that thinking twice is a smart way to avoid impulse purchases. Taking some time to think about a purchase will help you to decide whether the item is something you really need. Another way to do this is to have your spouse help you make a decision before spending a certain amount or more. For example, whenever my husband or I want to make a purchase that is over $200, we consult each other first for a second opinion.

Being smart with the gifts God has given you is a way to honor Him and thank Him. "Whoever speaks, is to do so as one who is speaking the utterances of God; whoever serves is to do so as one who is serving by the strength which God supplies; so that in all things God may be glorified through Jesus Christ, to whom belongs the glory and dominion forever and ever. Amen" (1 Peter 4:11, NAS).

Assess Your Talents

Consider where you have talent and how you could use that talent to bring in some income. Could you start a home business or do part-time work that differs from your current job? I chose to do several things with my home business, one of which included my love of writing. I did editing work for clients. This kind of work could be done in evenings and during the children's naptimes. It was a great way to add to our income and work around the children's schedules at the same time.

Don't Worry About What Everyone Else Is Doing

In our culture today, there is tremendous pressure to "be the best" and to "succeed." There are also constant advertisements trying to tell you that you need to buy "their" product, build one of "their" homes, or make a lot of money in order to be happy. Don't listen; concentrate instead on the necessities for your own family. You don't have to live up to "culture's expectations," but you should do what is best for your family. "Do not let your heart envy sinners, but live in the fear of the LORD always" (Proverbs 23:17, NAS).

Remember that your choices should be about God's plan for your family, not what the culture expects.

> Stand firm then, with the belt of truth buckled around your waist, with the breastplate of righteousness in place, and with your feet fitted with the readiness that comes from the gospel of peace. In addition to all this, take up the shield of faith, with which you can extinguish all the flaming arrows of the evil one. Take the helmet of salvation and the sword of the Spirit, which is the word of God.
>
> —EPHESIANS 6:14-17, NIV

Consider a Spousal IRA for Your 401K Money

If you are putting money away for retirement, which I recommend highly, you can increase your retirement funds by contributing up to $4,000 a year (as of 2005) into a separate spousal account. This is an option if there is only one spouse who is working. In many families, all $4,000 allowed may not be possible per year, but any money in savings is better than no money in savings. A financial advisor could give you more information on this kind of account.

Design a Family Plan

Take some time to consider the planning that your family needs to do. Go through each of the items in this chapter and take notes. Talk them through with your spouse, and begin to plan *before* your precious ones arrive on the scene. For those of you who already have children, you can still look back and consider how you need to make changes to your financial habits.

Also, spend time in prayer for your family needs. "Or what man is there among you who, when his son asks for a loaf, will give him a stone? Or if he asks for a fish, he will not give him a snake, will he? If you then, being evil, know how to give good gifts to your children, how much more will your Father who is in heaven give what is good to those who ask Him!" (Matthew 7:9-11, NAS). God knows your needs already, but He still wants you to spend time talking to Him about your specific hopes for your family.

Try Not to Get Overwhelmed

Perhaps as you read through this chapter you felt overwhelmed, thinking that there are so many suggestions that you *could do* that you don't know if you can do them all. Make a list or start with the ones that seem the easiest to try. Try to pick two of the suggestions from this chapter and focus on those first. Then work toward the other suggestions; by the time you accomplish a few, the ones that are left may not feel so overwhelming anymore.

Dear Lord,

Some of us have skills in planning, and many of us don't. Whichever type I am, please help me to plan well for my family. Help me to research well, consider options with discernment, and make good, solid decisions for our family. Please be with me every step of the way, Lord. Amen.

CHAPTER 4

Can You Afford to Work?

By wisdom a house is built, and by understanding it is established.

—Proverbs 24:3, NAS

There can be a lot of "costs" to working. These costs can really add up, thus depleting your take-home pay.

In the worksheet below, take some time to determine the costs per year that you spend on taxes, vehicle costs, etc. There is a sample for a salary of $40,000 to help you. After completing this form, you should be able to see how much of your salary you really get to use after paying for your work expenses.

Type of Work Expense	Example for Salary of $40,000	Your Cost Per Year
Federal income taxes, Social Security, and Medicare tax (15% of total)	$6,000	
Social Security and Medicare tax (7.65% of total)	$3,060	
State income tax (3% of total)	$1,200	
Child care	$10,000 (based on $200/week for 50 weeks)[1]	
Car payments	$3,000 (based on $250/month)	
Car insurance	$1,200	

(continued on next page)

Car fuel and maintenance ($0.585/mile – U.S. federal allowance as of September 2008)	$4,885 (based on 33.4 miles/day for 50 weeks)[2]	
Work clothes, dry cleaning, and other professional appearance costs	$750	
Lunches out	$2,500 (based on $50/ week for 50 weeks)	
Convenience foods rather than cooking (i.e., frozen dinners/processed foods)	$1,000	
Ordering food or dining out rather than cooking	$3,000 (based on 2 days per week at $30, 50 weeks per year)	
Gifts, special occasions for work parties	$300	
Housekeeping help	$1,400	
Other		
Salary	*$40,000*	
Total Work Expenses	*$38,295*	
Actual income (Salary – total work expenses)	$1,705	

Dear Jesus,

As we look at our family finances, give us the insight we need. Guide us as we consider all of the financial needs we face. Help us to be diligent and thorough with our money management and to remember not to idolize money and the things it can buy. Instead, let us remember what You told us in Jeremiah 29:11: "'For I know the plans that I have for you,' declares the Lord, *'plans for welfare and not for calamity to give you a future and a hope.'" Amen.*

CHAPTER 5

Determining Your Budget

After we were married, we agreed to base our lifestyle on my husband's paycheck and to try to put my paycheck in savings as much as possible. That helped us to make the decision for me to stay at home when our first son was born. The transition to being parents and all that goes into that lifestyle change was easier because we did not live a day-to-day lifestyle based on two paychecks.

—Teacher and Former Stay-at-Home Mom

Our choices about our lifestyles will have a significant impact on our finances and the possibility for being an at-home parent. Below is a worksheet designed to help you determine your budgetary needs each year.

Follow the instructions to finish this worksheet:

1. In the first column is the budget item. There is room in this column toward the bottom for you to add items that might not be listed here already.
2. In the second column, enter the amount you would need per year for each item.
3. After filling out the costs per year, look at the last two columns. First, find everything that is critical to the survival of your family and put a checkmark in the "Need" column.
4. Then put a checkmark in the "Want" column for the remaining items.
5. Look at the "Wants" and decide which you can cut from your budget.

Budget Item	Cost per Year	Need	Want
Mortgage/rent			
Taxes (if not already included in mortgage)			
Home insurance (if not already included in mortgage)			
Electric bill			
Gas bill			
Water bill			
Sewer bill			
Telephone bill			
Cell phone bill			
Home maintenance			
Other home-related costs			
Life insurance			
Medical insurance			
Dental insurance			
Eye insurance			
Co-pays for doctor visits, prescriptions, etc.			
Car payments			
Car insurance			
Automotive personal property tax, registration fees			
Car fuel and maintenance ($0.585/mile, U.S. federal as of September 2008)			
Student loans			
Credit cards and store cards			
Child support/alimony			
Clothes			
Food			
Pet costs (i.e., vet appointments, pet supplies, etc.)			
Dining out			
Lunches			
Cable and online service			

Videos/DVDs, CDs, magazines, newspapers			
Vacation(s)			
Hobbies/interests			
Haircuts and other personal grooming (i.e., nails, etc.)			
Dry cleaning			
Gifts for holidays			
Gifts for birthdays			
Emergency money			
Savings			
Other: ______ ______ ______			
Total expenses:			

Dear Lord,

Sometimes in our daily life it is hard to remember the difference between what we "want" and what we truly "need." As we complete this worksheet, help us to determine where we can stop spending money and how to better manage the gifts You have given us. Help us to remember that every good gift comes from Your hand (James 1:17). Amen.

CHAPTER 6

Savings From Reducing or Eliminating Work Hours

> Staying at home full-time and working part-time were the best decisions I made for myself. Although there have been many sacrifices and changes to adjust to, I consider myself very fortunate to continue to work and be there full-time for my son. It certainly is not easy, and it can be very difficult to manage at times, but the value of being home full-time to raise my son outweighs all of the challenges.
>
> —Senior Graphic Designer

When I received my survey responses for research for this book, 67 percent of the respondents said that they made financial sacrifices to be home more with their children. One significant encouragement, however, is that when you reduce or eliminate your work hours, there will be some savings that occur.

Vehicle Savings

There are several ways money spent on your vehicle can be saved when you reduce or eliminate work hours. The first way is by reducing the amount of gas you use to get to and from work. Your vehicle mileage will be lower, and this can be a significant amount of money if you have a long commute by car. My commute to work was about thirty-five minutes; half was in highway miles. I immediately noticed a difference in the amount of money I was spending on gas.

As you put fewer miles on your vehicle, you are also reducing the amount of wear and tear on your vehicle. Wear and tear will happen, but the less you have your vehicle on the road, the less wear you should see. By reducing the miles driven, you will also reduce the frequency of oil changes, maintenance, and tune-ups, which will definitely prolong the life of your vehicle investment.

Generally, if you drive less than three days per week to work, your insurance company will charge you a lower rate, calling it a "pleasure rate" rather than a "to work rate." This means that they'll be charging you for pleasure use of your car only, because you drive to work fewer than three days a week.

One way families have seen enormous savings has been by eliminating the need for two vehicles. Some of the survey respondents said that they no longer had a need for two cars, and that saved them both annual insurance costs and a car payment every month. Our family did not do this because I needed the second vehicle for my project work for clients and for errands, but my husband's truck was paid off, so we only had one car payment to deal with.

Clothing Savings

I went from wearing business casual at work every day to the occasional business suit for client meetings. We used the dry cleaner about six times a year instead of every other week. This was a huge money saver for our family. When you work from a home office or don't work at any office, your dress code doesn't have to be as expensive as it does in a typical business office.

If you work fewer days or no days, you will be able to save money on clothing purchases. You won't find yourself going through as many pairs of panty hose, dress socks, and nice shoes because you won't be wearing them as often. Business outfits can be very pricey, and casual clothes can be much more reasonable to buy. It makes sense that you should see large savings from your wardrobe change.

In addition, you can coordinate your work clothes so that you don't have to own as many as you might working more hours at the office. Try to stick with certain basic colors and designs that you can rotate and mix together for different outfits.

Child-care Savings

Good day care tends to be expensive, but even if you find an option that is not what you consider to be expensive, you will still pay a lot more for some form of child care every day instead of just once in a while. In addition, most child care locations will charge per child, so when you have baby number two, you've doubled your expenses and therefore lowered the impact of the second salary within your home even more. In addition, some day care centers require payment/contracts for five days a week, and you pay even if your child is home sick or on a holiday, or if you only want four days a week of care.

Children are more prone to get illnesses at day care. Even if the day care is very clean, you can't prevent children from wiping their hands on their faces and spreading their cold germs around. Because children will get more illnesses while in day care, you will probably spend more on doctor's visits and medicines, and you will need to use personal time off from work.

Food Savings

As much as I tried to make my lunch every day when I was working full-time, it didn't happen. After children arrived, that would have become an even lower priority on my "to do" list. When you are at a workplace, you don't have the luxury of a cupboard full of options and a refrigerator full of leftovers to grab when you need lunch. So you'll be stuck with the reality of buying lunch often…a very expensive reality over time.

In addition, one of you staying home from work makes it much easier to help the employed spouse by making lunches and/or reminding them that there is food in the refrigerator that they can take to work for lunch. Just by reducing the number of lunches that my husband eats at restaurants while working saved our family $40 a week, or $2,000 a year!

Tax Savings

When you lose one income, it might move your family into a lower tax bracket. This can be a big impact on the amount of taxes you pay every year. Ask your financial advisor for information on how your tax bracket can impact the amount of taxes you pay per year.

Dear Lord,

Wisdom is what our family needs as we consider how to best save and use money. Inspire us with ideas, and guide us through our management of the gifts You have given us, including our earnings. Help us to be thankful for the blessings in our life and to use discernment as we provide for our children. Amen.

CHAPTER 7

Ways to Save Money

Every good gift and every perfect gift is from above.

—James 1:17, NKJV

Some of the most valuable information that came from the survey respondents were the suggestions they gave on ways to save money. These were families that had been through the process of living on less, and their suggestions were creative and practical.

I compiled their suggestions and combined them with a list of my own ways to save money. Take time to consider ways you are already trying to save money, and then look at the items you haven't tried yet. You might find some great money savers to fit your family.

Cost-Savings Ideas

Check off the items that you have already started to do.

Food

- ❑ Eat meals out less and cook at home more.

  One suggestion to help put this into practice is to make twice the size when you make a meal and then freeze half for another day. I often make two lasagna meals or two chicken and rice dishes, and then I freeze one of them. This helps me to buy items in bulk, which in the long run typically costs less.

- ❑ Buy produce at a local farmers' market rather than at a food chain/ supermarket.

  Find out about the closest and most accessible farmers' market in your area. The closest one might be near your home on weekends, but there could also be one close to your work location on weekdays. Take advantage of your lunch break if this is the case, and visit the one by your work.

- ❑ Prepare homemade lunches for the spouse who is working full-time and for your children.

  I often buy lunch items in bulk, such as granola bars, juice boxes, and plastic sandwich bags. I place these lunch items together in the cupboard so that it speeds up the process when I'm making several lunches at a time. I open the cupboard with the items that do not need to be kept in the refrigerator, and within moments I have several items ready for our lunch boxes.

- ❑ Compare food prices rather than just buying what you always have bought in the past.

  Doing this well can take some time. Rather than overwhelming yourself by trying to compare prices for everything on one trip to the grocery store, set a goal to compare prices for the products in one section of the store with each visit. You can focus on dairy products one day, meat products another day, frozen products another day, and so on.

- ❑ Pick fruits yourself when possible.

  Berry picking can be fun with your kids, and then you can freeze the fruit for winter. Look up information on how to best freeze fruits and vegetables, since different methods work best with different products.

  For example, to freeze blueberries, you first wash the blueberries gently in a colander. Then you place the blueberries on a flat cookie sheet and put the cookie sheet into your freezer. Give the berries at least an hour or so to harden individually. Once they are frozen, scrape the frozen berries off of the cookie sheet using a spatula, and place the blueberries into a freezer bag. Squeeze any extra air out of the freezer bag, and place it in your freezer. When you want some berries, you'll now be able to take out a few at a time, because they froze separately on the cookie sheet rather than freezing to each other in a clump.

- ❑ Shop the perimeter of the grocery store (meats, vegetables, dairy, bread) to avoid buying junk food and unnecessary items found in the center aisles.

  I often avoid certain aisles, such as the aisle with sodas and chips because I know that I don't *need* any items in that aisle.

- ❑ Use coupons.

  However, do not buy an item just because you have a coupon if another brand without a coupon is still cheaper. Watch the weekend paper for sale items you use.

  There are also Web sites that list coupons weekly. Research the best coupon Web sites for your family purchases.

- ❑ Look at the "cost per quantity" price on the shelf prices in the store when comparing similar items.

  For example, two brands of orange juice may be priced the same, but one is 2 quarts and the other is only 1.75 quarts. Therefore, you are getting less product in the 1.75 quart container for the same price.

- ❑ Become a member of a warehouse club to save on bulk items like diapers, paper products, soup, etc.

  Warehouse clubs typically have many products you might use regularly, and usually buying in bulk saves you money in the long run.

  However, do not buy products that you normally would not use in large amounts; that way you don't waste food items that you purchase in bulk.

- ❑ Cook from scratch rather than buying premade meals.

  This might be more intimidating for some people than for others. Being comfortable cooking new foods takes practice. Set realistic goals for yourself. If you have little experience in a kitchen, try to learn how to make one new thing per week. If you have more experience, try more new recipes.

You won't become a fantastic chef overnight, so don't expect that from yourself. Keep it simple and fun so that you don't become frustrated with cooking. Look up recipes online or buy a simple cookbook to use to give you ideas.

While you learn new recipes, you can also include your children in the process. It can be great fun for a child to help with simple tasks like pouring and mixing ingredients in a bowl.

A few examples of items or meals that are typically cheaper when you make them yourself are: homemade cookies, pancake mix, muffins, cupcakes, lasagna and hamburger patties.

❑ Make your own baby food.

Buy a food grinder, grind up whatever you eat (if you eat balanced meals), and give to baby too, if baby is ready. You can also grind food, put it into ice cube trays, and freeze it. The ice cube size is perfect for individual, baby-size portions. You can defrost or heat up the cubes when you're ready to feed them to the baby.

❑ Have a vegetable garden and do canning every year.

There are numerous books and Web sites dedicated to the art of growing hearty vegetables and canning both fruits and vegetables. Research the type of products that you want to grow and store. Items that you need for canning are usually sold in grocery stores.

❑ Nurse your baby to save on formula.

This is not for everyone, but for those of you who are physically able to nurse your child, it is a huge money saver. You can even freeze extra milk in your first few weeks after the baby is born, when your body is typically producing extra milk. Lactation consultants and pediatric nurses at your child's pediatrician can usually advise you on how to do this, as well as how long you can store the milk in the freezer.

If you are unable to nurse, you can try to save coupons for formula products even before the baby is born. However, you should wait before buying too many containers of formula until after the baby is born. Some babies have challenges with certain types of formula, so you'll want to see which type is best for your baby before stocking up on a lot of formula.

- ❑ Plan meals ahead for one week.

Only go to the grocery store after you've planned your meals for the week, and buy *only* what is on the list. When you plan your meals ahead, you can try to coordinate items that you need.

For example, if I am planning to make kielbasa and hamburgers in the same week, I'll also want to purchase one green pepper and one onion, and then I'll use half of each vegetable for each of the two meals.

- ❑ Serve water at meals instead of soda and apples instead of a bag of chips.

Often healthier is cheaper! Water is very important for your diet, and it is not as expensive as soda or juice.

Pay attention to what you are eating, and you might find ways to spend less *and* eat healthier at the same time.

- ❑ Try the store brands of food rather than always getting the more expensive name brands.

If you are not comfortable with this idea, try just one package of something in the store brand. If you don't like it, you haven't wasted a lot of money. If you do like it, you can buy that brand from now on, since it will almost always cost less.

- ❑ Do not shop when you are hungry.

When you shop hungry, everything will look delicious, and you will buy more than you intended. Try to eat a meal or at least a snack before going grocery shopping.

- ❑ Stock up on items when they are on sale.

There are two reasons for stocking up on items: (1) it will save you money over time, and (2) you won't have to run to the store for a single item; you will already have it in your pantry.

Start an inventory and price guideline a little at a time so that you don't get overwhelmed.

For example, we have an extra freezer, and I often have a list of the contents taped to the top of it so that I can keep track of what we already have in the house. This helps so that I don't have to go through the extra freezer each time I'm wondering about what we have in the house already. I can just look at the list on top of the freezer to see what is inside.

- ❑ Buy family packs of meat, grated cheese, etc.

  When you get back from the store with these larger portions, divide them into 1-pound portions (or whatever size you usually use) and then freeze them.

- ❑ Buy only freezer bags rather than storage bags.

  Freezer bags are much thicker and can be washed by hand or in the dishwasher. They can also be reused many times before they are worn out.

- ❑ Use "chip clips" to keep groceries that come in bags fresh.

  These clips work great at keeping items fresh for a longer period of time, helping you to prevent wasting food that goes bad quickly.

- ❑ If you have a bread maker, use it.

  You can save money and eat healthier bread when you make it yourself. If you use a bread maker, you can buy products such as flour, sugar, salt, and yeast in bulk to save costs over time.

  Making your own bread can also save you time and gas money when you don't have to make a trip to the store for "just bread."

- ❑ Take leftover pieces from bread loaves, cut them into small cubes, and freeze them.

  You can use these bread pieces for recipes that require bread crumbs or bread cubes, like stuffing and meatloaf. This works really well if no one in your family prefers the end pieces of the bread for sandwiches, or if you make your own bread and have pieces break off while slicing it. You can put those pieces in the freezer to use for a future recipe rather than throwing them out and wasting them.

Utilities

- ❑ Reduce or eliminate cable or satellite television, or change it to a basic option.

We buy basic cable, and the cost difference is over forty dollars a month. Different areas offer different services for cable and satellite television. Research the best deals in your area, and take advantage of them.

If you are trying to justify the cost of your cable bill, track your time using movie channels or other "non-basic" channels. If you do this for a month or two, you can look back and see how often you are using those extra channels.

- ❑ Remove unnecessary services from your phone service.

Are caller ID, 3-way calling, voice mail, etc. necessities for you, or can you have less features with a lower monthly bill?

When I went to purchase my last cell phone, I only needed the basic service. The cost was much lower than it would have been if I had chosen to include all of the features available.

Another option is to cancel your regular phone service and use just your cell phone.

- ❑ Only heat rooms that you use in your residence and/or install a programmable thermostat.

You may also be able to close certain vents in your home to force heat to the rooms that are largest and most difficult to heat.

- ❑ Drop off payments at close locations to save on stamps.

Your electric bill, gas bill, or house payments might be examples of payments you could make on your way to another location.

Several bills can be paid at our town hall, and I drive by the town hall often, giving me a reason to save a stamp or two each month.

Another possibility is to use online bank services such as bill pay to pay your bills. In this case you save on both postage and the number of checks you have to buy.

Home and Transportation

- ❑ If you buy a home, buy one that you can afford on one salary.

  If you can't afford a house on one salary, wait to buy one until you can. A home mortgage is a big commitment, and you have to consider if you will be able to meet this commitment for many years to come. Buying a home with a payment that requires both of your salaries to pay it will put you at serious risk if one of you loses your income.

- ❑ Review and revise your insurance policies (i.e., car, home owners, etc.).

  Consider your options, such as a higher deductible, which might give you a lower premium.

- ❑ Research refinancing your mortgage.

  Refinancing typically makes sense if you will be in your home for years to come. Consider how long you plan to be in your home, and look at the overall financial outcome if you refinance.

- ❑ Switch your electric and gas bills to "even billing" or "budget plans."

  This can help you to avoid winter price spikes, making it easier to plan for these monthly bills.

- ❑ If you can manage with one car, you reduce your car payments and insurance in one large chunk.

  If you reduce the number of cars you use, be sure to contact your insurance agent. Even if you are in the middle of the year, this can impact your overall payment.

- ❑ Rent an extra room to a family member or friend.

  This is a good idea only for those who have the space. You also want to consider the impact on your family relationships if you add another person to your household. Make this decision prayerfully and carefully, and do not make it in a rush.

- [ ] Do your own home improvements.

  You can take classes or do research on how to do many home improvement projects. You may also know someone else who is handy, who might let you "learn" from them.

  You can also consider ways to "trade" services with friends who are skilled at remodeling. You could offer babysitting help, yard work help, or other skills in exchange for their help in a remodeling project.

- [ ] Purchase furniture/housewares at consignment stores, or look in the newspaper.

  This might be especially helpful when you have a college student who needs furniture. When I was in college, I had very small requirements when it came to furniture needs. I even slept on a mattress directly on the floor in my first college apartment!

- [ ] Share lawn mowers and snow blowers with neighbors.

  I know of two sets of neighbors who actually bought a lawnmower together. They both helped pay for the mower, and took turns paying for maintenance needs for the mower.

- [ ] Check to see if you still owe private mortgage insurance (PMI) on your house.

  You'll no longer owe PMI once your equity has risen to more than 20 percent of the property value.

- [ ] Before making a home furnishing purchase, ask yourself some questions that will help you make a good decision.

  The questions to ask yourself include:
    1. Where will I put it?
    2. Where will I store it in off-season?

  If you don't have a place for it, don't buy it, even if you absolutely love it.

- [ ] Put deflectors on heat vents to direct the flow of heat across the floor instead of straight up to the ceiling.

Since heat rises, it will go straight up toward the ceiling. The irony is that people can sit and walk below the best heat in their homes, since warm air rises.

- ❑ Turn the hot water tank thermostat down as far as possible, within the manufacturers' recommendations.

  You'll have to test this out in your home to find a good temperature.

  You can also do your laundry in cold water whenever possible to save on hot water.

- ❑ If your windows are drafty in winter, cover them with plastic.

  It might also be more cost efficient to replace your old windows. New, high quality windows can help lower your heating or air conditioning costs over time.

- ❑ Don't throw out old washcloths—turn them into cleaning rags.

  Use them instead of paper towels to clean up spills on the floor, for dusting, for washing windows, etc. You'll find that you use a lot less paper towels.

- ❑ Turn off all lights when not in use.

  Take time to teach your children about this money saver as well. By teaching your children to turn off the lights when they leave a room, you're helping them to make a difference too.

Financial Management

- ❑ Plan your finances for a family *before* you have children, if possible.

  If you already have children, you can still do good planning. Start planning for your family's financial health immediately using the budgeting tool and other financial ideas in this book.

- ❑ Don't carry any balances on your credit cards.

  If you owe on your credit cards, pay them off *first*. Credit card debt can skyrocket quickly.

- ❑ When making a purchase, determine whether it is truly a *need* or a *want*.

  If it is a *need*, it should be a higher priority than a *want*.
  Ask yourself these questions when making your decision:
  1. Does our family *need* this item to survive?
  2. Is this item something I *need* to buy or something I *want* to buy?
  3. If this is something I *want* rather than *need*, do I still have to pay for the items that our family *needs* first?

- ❑ Make an agreement with your spouse to never spend above a certain amount of money without consulting each other.

  This will help you to think twice before you make a big purchase. Decide on the amount of money you need to make agreements on together before you make any large purchases on your own.

- ❑ Determine how much it costs you to go to work and compare that to the amount of money you bring home.

  In many cases, you may not even break even, or it may be a minimal amount of income. Use the "Can You Afford to Work?" worksheet in this book to determine your work-related costs.

- ❑ Save money in advance of your child's birth.

  Even before your child arrives on the scene, your monthly costs will increase. Each new arrival to your family can mean more costs for formula, clothing, food, electricity, etc. throughout the year.

  One way to save this money is to direct deposit a portion of your earnings into a separate account that you designate as "money for the baby." You can start this account months before the baby comes and budget your household finances on the remaining money.

- ❑ See if your bank can link your checking and saving accounts so the combined total covers the minimum balance required.

  This can help you avoid monthly charges. Often banks that link the two accounts will allow one account to cover for another that may have less in it to prevent you having to pay a monthly fee for that second account.

- ❑ Take advantage of a flexible spending account if your spouse has access to one through work.

  Flexible spending accounts (FSA) reduce the amount of money you'll be taxed on at the end of the year. A flexible spending account is an account where you can put away pre-tax money to pay for co-pays and certain other medical expenses and preschool/nursery school.

  If your employer has this kind of an option with their benefit program, take advantage of it. Your employer will be able to give you the details of the program.

- ❑ If you get paid biweekly, there are two months per year that you will receive three checks during the month instead of two.

  Send that extra paycheck you receive twice a year to your savings account or to your mortgage company to pay down your mortgage. Also, be sure the extra payment is credited to principle, NOT interest.

- ❑ "Refinancing a mortgage or consolidating student loans to take advantage of low interest rates can cut monthly payments significantly."[1]

Clothing and Toys

- ❑ Do not walk the mall just to window shop.

  If you look, you might find something you feel that you "just have to have." If you don't see the item, you most likely won't think about purchasing it.

- ❑ Throw catalogs and store flyers away immediately.

  The flyers worth looking through first are:

  1. Those from discount stores in order to stock up on personal items such as toilet paper, paper towels, etc.
  2. Those that include coupons for items you are already planning to purchase.

- ❑ Share baby toys and clothes with family and friends.

  Before buying an item, I call my one of sisters, who typically gives me hand-me-downs for my kids. Rather than my buying items, she usually has something ready to give me. I then continue this process by giving the clothes my kids have grown too big for to my other sister.

- ❑ Buy toys and clothes at garage sales, consignment stores, or online.

  Many Web sites have many items that are sold "like new." Garage sales can also have items that don't have to be new to be useful.

- ❑ Only look on clearance racks. Walk right past all others.

  The clearance racks are typically toward the back of the store. Go there first before looking anywhere else in the store.

- ❑ Do not buy anything that needs dry cleaning (except suits).

  Dry cleaning is very expensive. For those clothes you already have that are dry clean only, consider using a home dry cleaning kit.

- ❑ Only buy an item of clothing if it meets ALL three of the following conditions:

  1. You absolutely love it.
  2. It is washable.
  3. It is on sale.

- ❑ Buy toys that last rather than just the "latest fad."

  Fads come and go, so think twice before buying a toy for your child to see if it is something all of your kids will get use out of. As the older child grows too big for it, will it still work or be fun for his or her younger siblings?

- ❑ Find out if there is a toy section at the library in your area.

  At the library near my sister's home, they have an entire area for children's resources. One section of the children's area has toys and puzzles children can use while at the library.

Miscellaneous

- ❑ Watch your spending on "luxury" items.

  This is another time to think before you make a purchase to consider whether or not the item is a *need* or a *want*.

- ❑ Make homemade gifts for holidays and birthdays.

  Ideas for homemade gifts include quilts, cross-stitched towels, wooden toys, family photos, homemade baked goods, jars of ready-to-make baked good ingredients, etc.

- ❑ Visit state parks and local sites instead of taking more expensive trips.

  Taking small day trips with your children can be fun and less expensive than out-of-town vacations. Go to towns or cities within an hour or so, check out the local games, or spend the day at the zoo. You can often find information on parks and other locations and activities on Web sites about your local area.

- ❑ Often when states have a "tax free" week on clothing, diapers are included, so stock up on diapers during those weeks.

- ❑ Travel by car for vacations to visit family and friends who live in interesting places.

  Staying with your extended family gives you the opportunity to spend time together as well as save money on hotels.

- ❑ Trade babysitting services with friends and family.

  Some couples who swap babysitting services with their friends often have children who are similar ages who look forward to getting together with their playmates.

- ❑ Rent movies instead of going to movie theaters, or go to your local library.

  A movie from a rental store or from the library costs less than individual tickets for your whole family to go to a movie at the theater.

Popcorn at home also costs less than at the theater, and then you get to choose how much butter you want!

- ❑ Use hair color and other hair products from the store rather than from a salon.

  This can take some practice, so be sure to research the product and color that will work best for you.

- ❑ Get and use a library card.

  Instead of purchasing books, magazines, videos, CDs, DVDs, and newspapers, go to the library once a week and borrow items. Libraries also have many free and fun programs for kids. I often list good children's books and movies that our family has enjoyed on my blog. You can find a link to my blog at: www.ditchthe.com

- ❑ Do fun but free stuff with your kids.

  Examples of these are library classes, going to playgrounds or parks, having a picnic, going to a beach, and hosting play dates.

- ❑ Do simple dates with your spouse.

  Dates with your spouse are important for your relationship, but they don't have to be extravagant. Have some simple and cost-effective dates, such as long walks, bike riding, and going out for ice cream.

- ❑ If you know you'll be giving a lot of gifts for kids' birthday parties, buy gifts in bulk when you spot great deals.

  The clearance area of stores often have items like this available. Each time you go to the store, check out the clearance aisle. This can be a great place to find gifts at half the cost or less. Before purchasing something, however, make sure it is something that will make a great gift.

- ❑ Make your own wrapping paper by painting or coloring plain white paper.

  Rolls of paper work great for this. This is a fun project for kids as well. Other ideas are to use newspaper comics for gift wrap and to reuse gift paper, tissue paper, and gift bags.

- ❑ Buy boxes of cards, or make your own.

  Boxes of cards are available for birthdays, anniversaries, and other special occasions. When you buy boxes of them, it is less expensive per card than when you buy just one card at a time.

  You can also make your own cards, either by hand or on the computer.

- ❑ Don't throw away that "empty" container of hand lotion, shampoo, etc. when you think it is empty.

  Cut off the top, and you will be amazed at how much is still inside, often enough for several days' use.

- ❑ Put bar soap in a spot where it will not get wet from the showerhead, as the water washes away the soap.

  By keeping the soap in a dry spot, the soap will last much longer.

- ❑ Do not buy liners for small trash cans.

  Use leftover grocery bags instead.

- ❑ Stop the dishwasher between the rinse and dry cycles.

  Open up the dishwasher, wipe excess water off the cup bottoms, and let the dishes air dry. This saves electricity.

  Many dishwashers come with an "air dry" feature. If you have this feature, use it.

- ❑ Don't buy kitchen gadgets unless they are *really* something you will use.

  Unused gadgets are not only a waste of money, but they also take up space unnecessarily.

- ❑ Don't get a clean bath towel every time you take a bath.

  Since you are clean when you use the towel, use it for at least three days before you get a clean one.

- ❑ Cut dryer sheets in half during winter months; in thirds (or don't use at all) during the summer.

  One-third of a sheet works just as well as a full sheet.

- ❑ Hang laundry to dry instead of using the dryer.

  In the warm months, or if you live in a warm climate, clothes that dry outside smell great.

- ❑ Save all those "reply" envelopes that come in the mail.

  Save the extra envelopes and use them for when the kids need field trip money and permission slips for school. You can send in the money or information in those envelopes rather than using your other envelopes for mailing items.

- ❑ Save small boxes to use as drawer dividers and storage containers for toys.

  Children's toys can quickly overtake a house. Using small containers helps your kids to keep their toys in sets that they come with. You can use shoe boxes, for example, rather than buying plastic containers.

- ❑ Shop around for prices on hair styling.

  The cost of highlighting your hair, for example, can range significantly between hair dressers. Also, you can consider checking out the local beauty school.

- ❑ Consider buying a family membership to a local zoo or museum in place of a different holiday gift.

  A family membership to a favorite place can get you access to activities all year long.

- ❑ Check out college, university, and technical school offerings.

  If you live near colleges, universities, and technical schools, they may offer services at a discounted rate. Their students get to learn skills on real people, and you can typically get a cheaper price for the service. This might be true for schools that offer dental care, hair care, massages, and other services.

Dear Lord,

There are some ways we can make changes to save money. Please give us strength and patience as we make these small but important changes. As we struggle with some of these adjustments, help us to remember to look to You for encouragement by hearing Your promise to us: "I have loved you with an everlasting love" (Jeremiah 31:3, NAS*). Amen.*

CHAPTER 8

The Impact of Changes in the Business World

> "For I know the plans I have for you," declares the LORD, "plans for welfare and not for calamity to give you a future and a hope."
>
> —JEREMIAH 29:11, NAS

Times have changed for the better, according to my colleague Carole Bellanca, PhD, from Bidwell Associates. "I think there are many fine companies that are willing to do whatever it takes to keep valuable employees who are struggling with their multiple roles. Times have changed, and the situation is much better now than it was twenty-five years ago. Then, we never mentioned having children in the workplace. There was no empathy. It was very difficult," said Bellanca. "Choice is a wonderful thing," she concluded, when considering how acceptance has evolved within the workplace.

In order to utilize the talents of parents who want to work part-time hours, businesses will need to become more flexible in their hiring and scheduling.

When I left my full-time job, the team that I left had only full-time employees. Four years later, there were several part-time mothers on the very same team. The company had adjusted their flexibility in order to retain quality talent.

Many companies have started making adjustments to their scheduling and flexibility in order to accommodate employees they don't want to lose or to get employees who have special schedule requirements to accept employment.

Businesses should become more flexible in their hiring process. "One legacy of the dot-com era is that nonlinear career tracks are more accepted and employers are less put off by a résumé with gaps and zigzags."[1] A résumé with a work gap may not have been considered in the past, but now hiring managers are learning that they need to be realistic...parents often leave the workforce for several years when they have young families. This is a reality that will not go away.

Overall, businesses have started to adjust in order to accommodate employee's situations because of the need to get and keep quality employees:

> It is why the accounting firm Deloitte & Touche has more than doubled the number of employees on flexible work schedules over the past decade.... It is why I.B.M. employees can request up to 156 weeks of job-protected family time off. It is why Hamot Medical Center in Erie, PA, hired a husband and wife to fill one neonatology job, with a shared salary and shared health insurance, then let them decide who stays home and who comes to the hospital on any given day. It is why, everywhere you look, workers are doing their work in untraditional ways.[2]

After doing research on this topic, the authors of *From Culture Wars to Common Ground* "propose a model not exceeding a sixty-hour work week for a mother and father that could be divided between the partners as thirty-thirty or forty-twenty."[3] If this recommendation was considered seriously by an employer, they might reconsider how they have structured their work process and explore how they could hire an employee for thirty hours instead of forty hours, or two employees for twenty hours instead of one employee for forty hours. "The equivalent of a job-and-a-half—this is what millions of families with young children want and need."[4]

"Society and organizations can no longer ignore the basic fact that high-achieving women have children. Alterations need to be made in order to keep them in the work environment....Professional mothers need reduced-hour jobs and careers that can be interrupted."[5] Businesses are already exploring ways to be flexible with current and future employees. Whether you are looking to go to part-time hours or are concerned about reentry into the workforce after your children are older, the flexibility that is being required of businesses is in your favor.

Dear Heavenly Father,

Sometimes I feel so small and insignificant in this world. The busyness and push to be "the best," which is such a strong part of our culture, can pull me in so easily, and I feel overwhelmed. Please help me to remember that You are constantly with me. Help me to see the opportunities in my work life so that I can make good decisions for my family. Open the heart of my current employer or future employer so that I can talk with them about a work schedule that our family can manage. Give me courage and support as I approach others with my ideas. Amen.

CHAPTER 9

Proposal for Your Company

If you are considering going to part-time hours in your current job but are unsure how to appeal to your employer, think carefully about your approach. The last thing you want to do is to have an unplanned conversation about this important decision.

If you are serious about wanting to go to part-time hours, and you want to see if your employer is willing to let you do that, spend some time researching how it will benefit your employer. For example, does your employer save a significant amount of money by paying for less benefits for part-timers? Is your employer going through hard times and trying to find ways to use fewer staff for projects? Does your employer need someone in a specialized role that you could fill on a part-time basis? Will there be fewer distractions for you if you are working from home, so you can work more efficiently? Consider your employer's needs, because this will help you in your approach.

Next, you will want to put together a formal proposal. The more prepared you are, the more confident you will be when you talk to your employer about why you think you can still be of benefit to them on a part-time basis. On the next few pages, I've provided a sample template for a proposal that you can use as a starting point. Use this sample to design your own proposal, keeping your employer's specific needs in mind.

The Next Direction in Our Relationship: Retaining Through Flexibility

Proposal for *ACME, Inc.*

From Sally Smith
July 25

What I am proposing

I am proposing to change my status from a full-time employee to a part-time employee. Following is a proposal to make that transition, considering the benefits and challenges for ACME.

I propose that I reduce my hours at ACME to two days a week immediately after my maternity leave. After three months, I propose that we determine if my hours could be increased with additional time working from my home. I see excellent possibilities for me to do work from my home office because of work I can do on the computer.

ACME's needs

ACME currently employs me in a full-time role. Through creativity, flexibility, and resourceful means, we can determine where my role can still service ACME with the most impact. I understand that my team has goals to meet and that I can have a positive impact on those goals.

Benefits to ACME

Saving money

- The average company pays 30 percent of salary for benefits. This percentage will be reduced for my part-time status, therefore saving ACME money.

- The costs of replacing key employees can average between 70 percent and 200 percent of the employee's annual salary. Because I will still be working at ACME and will not require training as a new hire would, there would not be the same replacement costs.

- Compensation for a suitable replacement can be 15 percent to 35 percent more than that of the employee he or she replaces. A full-time replacement would not be needed for me, again saving costs for ACME.

- I have already been trained to do my current job. ACME would save the costs of sending a full-time replacement through new hire orientation and job specific training.

Relationships

- Because I have already worked for ACME, I have had the opportunity to build strong relationships with employees. Strong relationships between employees make us a more effective team.

- Because I have been an employee at ACME already, this will be an excellent opportunity for ACME to explore telecommuting roles within the company. It is less of a risk than having a new employee telecommute. In order to telecommute, I would need access to a phone, a fax machine, and a computer with Internet access.

Projects I can do on a part-time basis

- Participate in team meetings via the phone if necessary
- Special projects
- Sample
- Sample

Projects I can do on a part-time basis for other teams

- Sample
- Sample
- Sample

Requests for compensation/equipment/supplies

Compensation

- Current hourly wage
- Health-care options
- Additional benefits that apply
- Participation in appropriate training and development
- Reimbursement for long distance phone calls and faxes made from my home office

Equipment

- Maintenance support
- Network connection from home
- Headset and phone connection, if necessary
- A workspace for me to get work done at the office

Supplies

- Supplies necessary for work at home (i.e., folders, paper, etc.)

Challenges and how to overcome them

Certain challenges will arise in any job. Below I've listed some of the challenges that came to mind when considering this proposal and some suggestions for how we can address these challenges proactively.

Home office set-up

- I plan to…

Concerns over my schedule

- We could…
- A communication plan to all employees could include information on my new role, my schedule, and information on how to contact me.

Some work can only be done at the office

- Although I would like to do work from my home office when possible, I know that some work (i.e., teaching classes, client presentation) can only be done at ACME. I would like to have agreement on the flexibility to do work at home when possible.
- We could set up regular meetings where I come to the office or phone in to be sure that our communication lines are kept open.

Additional options to explore

- If part-time work does not seem to be an option, I am open to considering doing contract work for ACME. However, I would prefer to stay with ACME as an employee.

Plan

1. I would return to work for ACME two days a week.

2. Three months after I've returned to work at ACME, we could determine if additional hours would work for both ACME and myself from my home office.

3. I would continue to receive an annual evaluation from my supervisor to let me know my progress and plan my goals for the next year.

CHAPTER 10

Keeping in Touch

> If someone is going from working full-time to being a full-time stay-at-home-parent, it is very important for them to find something to get involved in so that they still feel connected to the outside world.
>
> —PART-TIME PRESCHOOL TEACHER

One of the most challenging parts of changing my work hours from full-time to part-time was the lack of time spent with other adults. It took me a few months to get used to my new schedule and a few years to build a network of colleagues with whom I would keep in touch regularly. I am definitely a "people-person," and I missed my work colleagues and our conversations that often stretched me and helped me to grow intellectually. Initially, to compensate for the lack of adult conversation, I found that I talked nonstop when my husband got home from work, which nearly drove him crazy!

A positive outlook on life will help you to be a better parent, and your whole family will benefit. One of the ways to be more positive is to spend time with other adults.

> Many stay-at-home parents say they initially find it difficult to adjust to the round-the-clock demands of kids. Some say they miss the structure and predictability of the workplace, as well as regular interaction with other adults.[1]

I loved my babies, and I enjoyed them as toddlers too. Yet I needed to connect with other adults. There were many ways I was able to do that.

Spending Time With Other New Parents

I took advantage of my flexible schedule to network with other new parents. Spending time with these other new parents was valuable time for me as I learned how to raise my children. We would share stories and ideas and break into laughter over our children and their antics. Hearing about their concerns and frustrations helped remind me that I wasn't the only one who struggled with being patient or with keeping up with all of the daily chores. Some of the best ideas I heard came from those times with other parents, from potty training tips to ideas for child-friendly recipes and fun learning activities.

Here are some ways to network with other parents and with friends:

- Start a "parents at home" playgroup or join one that already exists. Make an effort to meet other at-home parents. Other at-home parents may be found in toddler story hours at the library, YMCA, church groups, etc.
- Brainstorm friendships you already have that you would like to build upon even more. Make an effort to build those friendships that you really want to see blossom. Invite other parents and their children to your home, and call those friends regularly to schedule get-togethers.
- Attend local parenting classes.
- Join an online association for stay-at-home parents.
- Join a preschool group. Many churches have preschool groups that you can consider joining.

Take Advantage of Technology

Technology has opened a huge door for parents. You don't have to be limited by location and time zones anymore. A friend of mine stays in touch with her sister who lives two time zones away by e-mail. She writes her sister regularly, and they are able to stay in touch better than they could if they had to only call each other between certain hours of the day.

There are blogs on the Internet that focus primarily on parenting. I started a blog that focuses on ideas for parents, and I often visit blogs of other parents sharing their ideas. For a link to my blog you can go to: www.ditchthe.com

I found technology also to be a great help to my business. Because of technological advantages, the phone and e-mail have made it possible for me to communicate with clients at any time of the day. I can respond to work requests in the evening and have a finished product waiting for them in their e-mail inbox when they enter their office the next morning. I can send reminders and questions to clients without having to worry about my children making too much noise while I'm on the phone by either leaving clients a voice mail message after hours or sending an e-mail or fax. Once I have taken the time to develop a relationship with clients, I have never found a client resistant to using e-mail as a main form of communication. In fact, many prefer it.

Take Advantage of Your Accomplishments

Before you leave a job, it is a good idea to get letters of recommendation that you can use in a future job search. Getting the letters of recommendation right when you are leaving means that the people you ask will have a clear memory of what you have accomplished.

The people you ask to write the letters of recommendation should:

- Know what you have accomplished while you were employed by the organization
- Know what your skills are
- Have competent writing skills so that they can effectively describe your accomplishments and skills
- Are comfortable with the request of doing the recommendation for you.

If you wait until the next time you want to apply for a job to get your letters of recommendation, it might be more difficult for you to contact the people you would like to write the letters. It would also mean that as time passed, your co-workers or former bosses might not remember all of your accomplishments and skills.

The following might be people you want to consider for writing your letters of recommendation:

- Your manager
- Your co-worker(s)

- Your client(s) or customer(s)
- Your human resource team member(s)

Business and Professional Networking

If you are running a home business, networking can often make or break your success. In the beginning of my business, its success was dependent on leads through current clients and networking with colleagues. Some of the networking I did to stay in touch with colleagues included:

- Joining a consultant group where I could both share projects and leads
- Continuing my membership with a local association that I had been a member of for years
- Joining another association related to my field
- Scheduling lunches with former work colleagues
- Sending two e-mails a year updating some of my colleagues from my last company about my progress
- Sending holiday cards to my clients and colleagues

Brainstorm

Every situation is unique; however, each person can benefit from some time spent coming up with ideas. Take some time to think about your own situation. Brainstorm ways for you to stay in touch with other adults, and then take the time to make them happen. Brainstorming in this case means to take some time, perhaps an hour, to think of some specific ideas for you and your family to try and then to determine how you might take the first steps toward those ideas. Try to set a goal of coming up with at least three ideas to try in the next three months.

Community and Faith-based Support

Families are often drawn toward community centers and faith-based organizations when their children arrive. They see the benefits that their children can get from being involved with these programs. It can become a great outlet for the parents as well. For example, many churches provide support groups, parenting programs, volunteer opportunities, a sense of belonging, children's activities, family activities, and more.

Keeping in touch with other adults is just one way for you to feel more in tune with the outside world. This will help you to establish a more peaceful home because *you* will feel more contentment from having connections with other adults. Another way to nurture your family with a peaceful environment is covered in the next chapter.

Dear Lord,

As I try things that are new to me, such as reaching out to other parents or networking, give me courage. Help me to look for support in a faith-filled environment and to drink in Your Word with other believers. Help me to get refreshment from my time with adult friends to help me be a better parent. Amen.

CHAPTER 11

Keeping *Your* Sanity

> He gives strength to the weary and increases the power of the weak. Even youths grow tired and weary, and young men stumble and fall; but those who hope in the LORD will renew their strength. They will soar on wings like eagles; they will run and not grow weary, they will walk and not be faint.
>
> —ISAIAH 40:29-31, NIV

As you spend valuable time with your family, your goal to provide the most nurturing environment for your family will require that you have an amazing amount of patience and that you keep your emotions in check. You will need to accept that the transition time from working full-time to part-time or no hours may take some adjustment. You may feel emotions you did not expect to feel: resentment, relief, frustration, delight, loneliness, fear, blessed, etc. Needing an adjustment period is normal. There are steps you can take to try to ease this adjustment period for you and your family.

Prayer and Scripture

With any decision, both the solace of prayer and the fit of Scripture can help guide you to a decision that is best for your family. Before making any major decisions that impact you and your family, spend time talking to God about your decision. He will gladly listen to your fears, hopes, and confusion, and He won't ever get tired of you reaching out to Him for guidance.

You might wonder, "How will I know God's answer?" There is no guarantee that you will know His answer for you, but you can look for it by:

Listening

Spend quiet time praying and listening for God's answer. It is one thing to make a request, but it is another to quietly wait and really listen. Even if you don't physically hear God speak to you, He may simply inspire you with a feeling or an idea. Listening with an open heart is ideal while waiting for the Lord to give you guidance.

Reading the Bible

Paul wrote to Timothy, "All Scripture is God-breathed and is useful for teaching, rebuking, correcting and training in righteousness, so that the man of God may be thoroughly equipped for every good work" (2 Timothy 3:16-17, NIV). God will provide the answer in time if you listen for it and seek His Word for it. The Bible has provided answers for people since the day it was written.

Ask others to pray for you

If the decision you are trying to make is something you are comfortable sharing with others, ask someone whom you trust to pray for you. Tell them as much as you are willing to share so that your friend can say a specific prayer for you. "A friend loves at all times" (Proverbs 17:17, NIV). Good friends will include your decision in their prayers and support you. Christians are called to support each other, and this is a great opportunity for someone to be a good friend to you.

Prioritize

With your spouse, discuss and write out your priorities for your family. You can include:

- Time with your children
- Time with your spouse and the importance of your relationship
- Time for yourself
- Household duties and how to share them
- Financial goals
- Career goals
- Physical health
- Spiritual growth
- Education

This will help you have the same focus as a couple when you have difficult decisions to make. Knowing your priorities will help you to maintain that focus on those most challenging days with your children.

Within that list of priorities, be sure to set aside time alone with your spouse. When children enter the picture, life can get very busy, and you will only benefit from keeping your marriage bond strong through time together as a couple. Remembering the importance of your marriage will help you on days when you have numerous bumps in the road. Try to include date nights in your schedule regularly…even simple dates that are not expensive but give you time to be together as a couple.

While prioritizing, Matthew 6:33 provides guidance: "Seek ye first the kingdom of God, and his righteousness; and all these things shall be added unto you" (KJV).

Be Realistic

Once you've made the decision to leave work or reduce your work hours, you may be surprised at some of the emotional changes you may go through. "It is important to realize that struggling with staying home versus working is not a reflection of your love, dedication, or parenting abilities."[1]

You might find yourself struggling to find acknowledgment and support in different places than you used to in the workforce. Jobs outside of the home typically have reward systems that lend to your sense of self-esteem, such as regular paychecks, annual goals, bonuses, and recognition programs. These will no longer be the same for you, and it may take awhile before you adjust to different sources of feedback and support. "Outside of the physical and household changes that new parents are constantly adjusting to, developing a stay-at-home routine as well as coping with the lack of socialization, opportunity for praise and feelings of accomplishment are among the top issues that new parents face when they choose to switch from working outside of their home to staying at home."[2]

In light of this, it is important to remind yourself to take the transition to part-time or no outside work hours one day at a time. Don't become frustrated with yourself for struggling with your new routine. It will take time to get a new "groove" to your life, just as it does with any change. Knowing that you aren't the only one who is having trouble adjusting may be of some comfort, as will talking about some of those challenges with your spouse. Be realistic with your own personal goals, and don't push yourself too hard in the beginning.

You could even consider keeping a daily journal. You can look back at what you accomplished and be proud of the many decisions you handle daily regarding yourself and your family.

Check-in

Do a check-in with your spouse every six months or so to reevaluate your priorities and your financial and family goals. Sit down and share honestly with each other how the past six months have gone and how you think things might need to change for the next six months. This will give you time to discuss changes you need to make and goals you want to reestablish. Spend time asking each other:

- "Have we done a good job of prioritizing what is important for our family in the last six months? How might we do an even better job?"
- "How will our lives be different in the next six months? What do we need to anticipate in the next six months?"
- "Will our work, school, and/or volunteer schedules change in the next six months? How will that affect our family?"
- "What should we continue to do in the next six months that has worked well for us? What steps should we take in the next six months that we have not tried before?"

This check-in time can really help you maintain your sanity, because you take the time to redirect your time when necessary. Redirecting your time means that you:

- Pay attention to how you are spending your days, hours, and minutes
- Make sure that you spend time on your family's priorities first

After starting my business, each year my husband and I would spend time discussing my business and, when we had time, to work it around our family needs. Some months I would intentionally reduce the amount of time I would market my business so that work never became too overwhelming. This helped us to stay focused on the main goal of my being home to raise our children.

You can also keep your family and your priorities in your prayers regularly, asking God to help you make daily decisions that honor Him.

Challenge Yourself

I have heard people talk about their fear of staying home with their children and letting their "minds turn to goo" from not challenging themselves intellectually. Based on your attitude and where you take the adventure of raising your children, you can find yourself growing intellectually as you never have before.

You can spend hours keeping your brain in gear by reading challenging books, writing, and finding other outlets utilizing your creativity. If you leave the workforce, you can still learn about the industry that you left by reading trade journals. You can listen to books on tape while doing household chores or driving, and you can get business, education, or theory books from the library. In fact, by reading in front of your children, you'll show them that reading is of value in your home. I often look down from a book I'm reading to see my sons holding their own books and exploring them with delight.

Remember Why

Remind yourself about the personal advantages you and your spouse can look forward to now that your work hours have changed. When you have a frustrating day, it helps to remind yourself about why you made this life change. Perhaps you realized that it would provide a more peaceful and nurturing family environment for your family. Maybe there are days when you are more receptive to your spouse's needs because of the time you get together as a family. Or perhaps you cherish the time you reserve with your spouse when he or she is home for family time by completing errands when your spouse is working. "Stay-at-home parents enjoy benefits that can't be measured in dollars: a more relaxed pace of life and the satisfaction of knowing your children are getting your full-time attention."[3] There are many benefits to you working less so that you can spend more time raising your children.

> A related article in *Working Women* was titled "Superwoman's Daughters: They don't want your job. They don't want your life. All twenty-something

> women want is to change the way America works." It said women who are leaving the workplace can't be understood without considering how they were raised. "Generations are motivated by what they were deprived of as kids. For those under thirty years of age, they had far too little time with their parents. Therefore, younger women seem determined not to make that mistake with their own children."[4]
>
> There is nothing wrong with money or power. But they come at a high price. And lately when women talk about success they use words like satisfaction, balance and sanity. That's why a recent survey by the research firm Catalyst found that 26 percent of women at the cusp of the most senior levels of management don't want the promotion. And it's why *Fortune* magazine found that of the 108 women who have appeared on its list of the top 50 most powerful women over the years, at least 20 have chosen to leave their high-powered jobs, most voluntarily, for lives that are less intense and more fulfilling.[5]
>
> Reminding yourself of the reasons you chose to stay at home adds additional support to stay focused on all of your goals as a family.[6]

Now that you have considered the big picture issues surrounding your transition from full-time work hours to part-time or no hours, the next section will give you some more detailed ideas on how to remove some of the stress from your home as you make this transition. Stress will never go away completely, but when you manage stress better, your family will benefit.

Dear Jesus,

It is so easy to let life get out of control through too many commitments and trying to accomplish too much in a day. Help me to focus my efforts where they belong and to make time for my family, as well as time with You in prayer. Lead me as I set my priorities so that my choices are pleasing to You. Amen.

CHAPTER 12

Maintaining *Family* Sanity

> It was the best decision I ever made, despite comments from my friends who told me I should try to "do it all" because it "can be done" and I should "have a career of my own." If it can be done, do it. Your life will be less stressed.
>
> —Stay-at-Home Mom

Ideas for Less Stress at Home

When you are running a household, there are many ways that you impact your family by alleviating stress in the home. Less stress in your home will make it a place that your family wants to be and where they will grow together. When you reduce your work hours, you make it possible to do things that you might not have time for otherwise.

> Of the analyses we conducted to address the question of children's judgments of mothers in relation to feeling rushed when they are together, most are significant. Specifically, children are more likely to see their mothers positively if their time with her is calmer.[1]

Below are some ideas on things you can do that will help reduce stress at home.

Help the person who is working full-time

Household errands

By getting certain household errands done while your spouse is working, you save time for your family to be together to do fun things like playing games, reading books, and relaxing. Just a few of the household errands you can accomplish with the kids in tow are:

- Post office errands
- Groceries
- Dry cleaning
- Bank deposits
- Library
- Gift shopping

Appointments

Doctor appointments, dentist appointments, and vet appointments can all happen during the hours when your spouse is working. You can reduce the stress for your family by scheduling these appointments and taking your family members there for appointments.

You can also be the one to handle appointments for deliveries to your home for new appliances and installations. By being able to have a flexible schedule, you can be home when workers need access to parts of your home, rather than your spouse having to take off time from work to handle these appointments. This allows your spouse to save precious vacation/personal days for time with you and your children.

Administrative help

Every week, and sometimes every day, new bills come in the mail. Someone needs to pay them, and if you manage all of the bills being paid, that is one less thing for your spouse to have to do when he or she returns from work. This is a task that you can easily manage from home.

You could use a budget sheet like the one below to keep track of your bills:

Type of Bill	Due Date	Amount Owed	Paid
Gas bill	June 3	$44.75	✓
Electric bill	June 7	$101.71	✓
Phone bill	June 20	$65.83	

Occasionally, your spouse might need help with other projects, such as:

- Sending birthday cards to their family members
- Updating their résumé
- E-mailing or faxing information to a colleague
- Editing
- Computer work

Make lunches

Every time your spouse has a lunch already made and ready to take to work, he/she saves two things: time and money.

The time your spouse saves makes it easier for him/her to get family errands done during the lunch break and to get home earlier at the end of the day.

Ironing and laundry

When you get the laundry done for everyone, your spouse has clothing ready for each new day at work and spends less time frantically searching for a clean shirt in the morning! There were days when my husband had important meetings come up with clients when I would iron shirts in advance, making it less stressful for him to get to those important meetings.

There are ways you can help your home be a place of peace by stepping in to help when your spouse is overwhelmed. This doesn't mean the working spouse never does any of the tasks mentioned above, but it helps if one spouse manages them the majority of the time so that when the other spouse is home, there is more opportunity for family time. There were several times when my husband spent some time at the ironing board because that task was not getting done by me...it always seemed to come last on my priority list. But he never complained because he knew that I was trying hard to help him in so many other ways. He knew that I spent as much time as I could making life run more smoothly for our busy family.

Say No

In his book *Bringing Up Boys*, Dr. James Dobson says, "Busyness and family isolation aren't new problems, of course. Moms and dads have struggled to control the pressures of living since World War II, but their approach has changed. Most mothers in the fifties and early sixties gave priority to their families, no matter what the cost."[2]

You don't always have to attend every event. If your schedule feels too busy to you, it probably feels too busy to your whole family. Say no when you and your family members need time to slow down. Everyone needs a night at home to relax once in a while.

Also, remember that your child is still young and does not have to be a soccer star at the age of seven. I've heard countless parents talk about their child playing hockey, basketball, and other sports. Pick what your child is truly interested in himself, and let him or her try things one at a time. If your child does not seem interested, don't push him to play a sport just because it is *your* favorite pastime. Slow down...give your child time to grow up, and give her time with you...the time that is most important for your child.

Dear Jesus,

Please give me courage to say no when I need to...especially when my family needs me. And bring me patience to help my spouse who is working full-time. Help me to see that my commitment to our family means helping others. Help me to avoid selfish feelings and to focus on Your example of love when I choose my own actions. Remind me that "the fear of the Lord *is the instruction for wisdom, and before honor comes humility" (Proverbs 15:33,* nas*). Amen.*

Part 3

DEFENDING YOUR DECISION

CHAPTER 13

Assumptions We Face

> If any of you lacks wisdom, let him ask of God, who gives to all generously and without reproach.
>
> —James 1:5, NAS

Financial Assumptions

"I'd love to take my baby to a swim class, but the Saturday classes are already full. And the only other times they hold classes are during the weekdays for the *rich* people," said a mother I knew. She assumed that parents who were home with their children during the day were rolling in piles of money. She assumed wrong.

This kind of comment can be hurtful, and it shows the speaker is uninformed. It comes from an incorrect assumption that if you're a stay-at-home parent, your family is made of money. From the survey responses of parents who have cut back on expenses, made critical changes to their spending habits, and, in some cases, struggle to pay for special things such as vacations and brand-name cereals, I know that parents who choose to stay home with their kids are often not wealthy.

According to a study conducted in the mid-nineties "by sociologists at Cornell University, nearly three-fourths of 117 middle-income couples in upstate New York were found to be scaling back their work assignments for the sake of the children. They were taking more time off and, when necessary, they were lowering their standard of living to accommodate the loss of income."[1]

Another financial assumption is that if you are working, you are bringing home a significant financial contribution. In reality, however, that may not always be true. "Together, state, federal, and Social Security taxes can eat up 20 percent to 40 percent or more of your pay. And at $100 to $200 per week per child, on average, day care can consume most or all of the rest."[2]

For example, if you are in a position that pays $45,000 per year, after taxes and Social Security, your net income is approximately $31,500 per year. This equates to $606 per week take-home pay. Now, let's assume that you drive round trip forty minutes to and from work each day; that equals approximately $90 in gasoline and wear and tear (oil changes, insurance, etc.) on your vehicle. You might eat lunch out about three times a week, spending about $30 per week. Day care for two children might cost you about $300 a week. Clothes/dry cleaning costs are about $40 a week. Nights when you eat out because you don't feel like cooking happen about twice a week and cost you $50. Now, your $606 per week just turned into $96, or about $5000 per year. Add in a few little extras, and you can see how your earnings can disappear quickly.

Career Impact

Other assumptions can be just as off-target. For instance, there is the assumption that if you leave the workforce, your career will be ruined or will stagnate, or you will lose the respect of your peers. Is that what the culture is trying to say, or is that reality? It all depends on you and your creativity, desire, and your attitude about life. The apostle Peter wrote, "Therefore humble yourselves under the mighty hand of God, that He may exalt you at the proper time, casting all your anxiety on Him, because He cares for you" (1 Peter 5:6-7, NAS). Prayer is a way to tell God your fears about your career. Take your concerns to Him, and ask for His help in being creative and having the right attitude about life for the well-being of your family. Isaiah 41:10 says, "Do not fear, for I am with you; do not anxiously look about you, for I am your God. I will strengthen you, surely I will help you, surely I will uphold you with My righteous right hand" (NAS).

I left a full-time job but continue to "stay in the business" through networking, project work through my home business, reading journals, and keeping records of my project accomplishments. If I go to an interview someday for a full-time job, I will be prepared with a portfolio demonstrating what I have accomplished from a home office: doing my own accounting, marketing to clients, doing my own project management, maintaining professional relationships, etc. I haven't "given up" my career. I've simply taken time to learn something new. In my case, that's learning how to run a business, and that is a fantastic selling point for future employers.

If I did not have a business of my own, I could still keep track of my accomplishments in a similar manner. Many "non-paid" accomplishments demonstrate your skills to future employers, such as: coordinating a pre-school group, reading books, taking online classes, assisting with school fund-raisers, participating on committees at your church or your child's school, etc. Showing that you have made a contribution, even if it is not in a business setting, is a way to demonstrate your skills.

Another learning experience for me throughout my career change has been learning to trust in God's plan for my life. Trusting Him to help my husband and me to make the best decisions for our family has been a new experience for me in my walk with God. "So do not worry about tomorrow; for tomorrow will care for itself" (Matthew 6:34, NAS).

Do I fear that my career has been ruined, or is stagnant, or that I have lost the respect of my peers? No. I can assure you of that. From the responses to the surveys, I find that other parents feel that their careers are not going on a downward or backward spiral. Their full-time careers will be there when they get back, if they decide to go back.

Having been a manager, I know how important it is to rely on good people in your work team. If you were good at your job before having children, you will still be a valuable employee when you go back to work. You will simply be in a different role, in a different company, on a different team, but you will have the same strong work ethic you had in the past, and your manager will know it and appreciate it, even if he or she doesn't say so.

Lisa Belkin states:

> Women today have the equal right to make the same bargain that men have made for centuries—to take time from their family in pursuit of success. Instead, woman are redefining success. And in doing so, they are redefining work.[3]

Four women share their career impact experiences

Within the last twenty years, four mothers had very different experiences when they went from being at-home parents to full-time employment. Four women who completed my surveys relay their memories of returning to full-time work, and their stories follow:

Not so easy

The first mother is now a college instructor who was a stay-at-home-mom for eighteen years. She found entry into full-time employment a challenge. "The greatest challenge for me back in the eighties was finding employment without a degree and, probably more importantly, without actual experience on a résumé," she said. Now that she has a master's degree and a full-time position, she can lend her experience to others. She said, "Parents who leave their full-time jobs to raise a family will most likely encounter some level of difficulty upon reentry to the workforce down the road. I think they have to acknowledge that with wide-open eyes. But rather than becoming angst-ridden about what awaits them at some future time, they should revel in the courageous decision made in the present, to stay home with their kids! Parenthood is the greatest calling."

Some challenges

The second mother is currently a full-time teacher. Before returning to work full-time, she worked part-time for ten years while her children were young. "I went back to full-time because I was told that if I didn't, I would no longer have a job there," she said. "The only issue I had with my employer was that I wanted a little flexibility on starting and leaving times of fifteen minutes. He refused," she explained.

The third mother was working part-time for about ten years while her children were young. "Full-time evolved easily; I was needed and then able to fill the position in my same workplace," she said. However, her challenge was helping herself and her family to adjust to the change back to full-time hours. "I felt the separation from my family. I was used to being there for them," she said. Her family understood and "pitched in…my husband learned to cook, something I'm thankful for now, and he enjoys it too."

Recruited

Now a mid-level manager, the fourth mother didn't face any challenges from employers when she was ready to reenter the full-time workforce. When I asked her if she had a difficult time finding full-time work, she said, "No, I was recruited for the position." Her advice to other parents is to stay connected with your industry and area of expertise, stay enrolled in professional memberships, read industry magazines to stay current, and continue to network whenever possible.

These four women had very different experiences, and all of these experiences occurred well before 2010.

In recent years, the flexibility for returning parents has continued to improve. As I explained earlier, one of my former employers has already provided more flexible hours within just the last four years. Many organizations have begun to do the same, and the timing couldn't be better for parents who want flexibility.

Media Bias

We are surrounded by messages daily from many different forms of media. Billboards, magazines, television, radio, Internet, and other forms of media constantly try to sell us on products, ideas, and ways to live our lives.

Family messages are often sent through these media, and they are not necessarily messages that are for the good of the family. Messages like this can often be political in nature, stemming not from what is truly best for your family but from what is best for the group benefiting from the message. When hearing a message about families and children, it is critical to question that message by considering who will benefit from it. Don't assume because it is in print or spoken about on a "reputable" talk show, that it is accurate or what is best for you and your children.

As a parent, you should not only filter messages for your child when possible, but you should also constantly question the message being sent to you as well. Television and radio shows often interview subject matter experts on topics and refer to books with studies when trying to show that they have researched their material. But don't believe messages that come from the media just because they have some statistics to throw around. For example, when doing research for this book and for the class I taught before writing this book, I read many magazine articles, Web site articles, and books to find out more information. One example of a book I read was titled *Ask the Children: What America's Children Really Think About Working Parents* by Ellen Galinsky. This book was written in 1999, and I checked it out from the library because the title itself intrigued me. I use some quotes in this book that came from *Ask the Children*, and I found material in the book that explained some of the ways today's children feel about their relationships with their parents. So overall, I am glad I read it and feel it was of value to quote several times in this book. However, I also read it very carefully and did not include some of the data that I felt sent an inaccurate message. You see, the *title* of the book made me *assume* that children of all ages would be considered in the studies. I found, however, that my assumption was wrong. I very carefully read the following in the Introduction:

> Parent interviews were conducted on the phone by Louis Harris and Associates with a nationally representative sample of 605 employed

> parents with children 18 years old or younger in June 1998. A nationally representative sample of 1,023 children in the third through the twelfth grades were given a self-administered questionnaire during the English classes in April-May, 1998.[4]

After reading this small paragraph in the Introduction, I realized that the opinions of children from the age of one day up through seven years were *not* being represented in these studies. Although ages eight through eighteen are indeed children, in order to truly represent the opinions of *all children* about how much both parents working has an impact on their daily life, seven-year-olds and younger would have to be included. I was glad that I didn't just skip the Introduction, as many readers tend to do, because knowing how the studies were done was critical for me to really determine how accurate I felt the data of the research was within *Ask the Children*. Below are three quotes from *Ask the Children* that were mentioned in this book that I read *very differently* once I understood that seven-year-olds and younger were not included in author's research:

> In *not a single analysis* is the mother's employment status related to the way a child sees his or her mother or father. Neither is her working part-time or full-time. This clearly is one of our most important findings.[5]

> Because the debate about working and parenting has at times assumed that children fare differently in families in which the mother is employed compared to those in which the mother stays at home, we looked for a difference in the ways employed and nonemployed mothers are viewed by their children. There is none.[6]

Under a section titled "The Bottom Line," the author wrote:

> These findings from other research on children's development support our own findings on how children grade their parents: Whether or not a mother is employed has very little to do with how her children grade her.[7]

The three quotes above make very strong statements that, if taken out of context, could be twisted in the media in such a way that the data might not be shared accurately.

Information in the media regarding day care should also be scrutinized carefully. According to former day-care center owners William and Wendy Dreskin, "Some researchers and many advocates of full-time day care have claimed that studies prove that day care is harmless or even beneficial to children's emotional development, and this message has frequently been repeated in books and magazine articles. This is far from the truth."[8] The day-care industry will benefit from messages such as these, but will your child? Bias is nothing new in the media world:

> In the midst of the ongoing day care controversy, parents faced with the day care decision and those who have already placed their children in day care need to beware of self-serving research, pre-mature conclusions, and a heavy bias in the media....Almost all books and articles on choosing day care say that if a child cries after the first few days there is either something wrong with the day care situation or, if it is a good one, it is not the appropriate one for that particular child. Nowhere is it hinted that day care itself may be the problem, that children may cry or complain in the best of situations, because what they really want is to be with their parents.[9]

As parents making important decisions for our children, it is critical that we question what we hear and read, and make sure that we dissect studies rather than just believe them. As a parent, I find it more important to question what I read constantly, whether it is in book, newspaper, periodical, or other media form. I encourage all parents to use thorough analysis when reading anything that lists surveys, data, or research from studies.

Societal Pressures

Another challenge for us as parents is encountered from the beliefs within society. More often than not, what society pushes is not what is best for your family. "Society's attitudes are changing toward stay-at-home mothers. Working mothers of young children are a growing demographic and the traditional family structure is evolving to accept the role of working mother and wife. The stay-at-home mother is becoming less valued than before."[10]

This feeling of being undervalued can be very challenging for a stay-at-home parent. These parents are doing an incredibly important job...guiding other human beings toward adulthood.

If you find yourself frustrated by the lack of respect given for stay-at-home parents, it is important that you also realize that many do recognize the importance of that role. There are other stay-at-home parents, church leaders, children, and even some politicians who understand the critical role you play in making this world a better place. When my son hugs me after I read him a story and says, "You're the best mommy in the whole world," I find it easy to dismiss critics who would say my job is not of value. Don't allow society to make you question yourself or the importance of your presence in the daily life of your child. Your being there for your child is important, and you have a challenging, critical, and priceless job every day as you guide your own child toward adulthood.

Spend time in prayer and listen to God's plan for your life and for your family. By constantly looking to God for His plan in our lives, we can better focus our energy toward the things that matter the most, and one of those very important parts of our life are our children.

So, What About the Challenges You Face?

Take some time to consider how you can face cultural challenges and assumptions when making decisions for your family. Will you face difficult questions from your colleagues, friends, and family? Will you worry that your career is over? How will you address those challenges? By thinking through your answers now, you will be more prepared to face those challenges when they occur.

In addition, remember to ask God to be with you throughout your challenges. The journey through a difficult day will be calmer for you with God's support. "Pay close attention to yourself and to your teaching; persevere in these things, for as you do this you will ensure salvation both for yourself and for those who hear you" (1 Timothy 4:16, NAS).

Keep looking to the Lord for guidance daily so that it is natural and easy for you to call out to Him when difficult challenges happen in your life. God will hear you. "Just as a father has compassion on his children, so the LORD has compassion on those who fear Him" (Psalm 103:13, NAS).

Dear Lord,

Facing the assumptions that cause fear in my life can make me feel trapped and overwhelmed. Please help me to refocus on Your plan for my family and me. Help me to have a strong heart for You, my spouse, and my children. Please help me to see clearly through wrong assumptions rather than letting them keep me in fear. Thank You, Jesus, for Your constant love. In Your precious name I pray. Amen.

CHAPTER 14

The Reason for the Change

We love, because He first loved us.

—1 JOHN 4:19, NAS

One afternoon I put in a *Rescue Heroes* DVD for my son. As soon as the opening song accompanying the action scenes with the heroes began to play, my son started to dance around the room as he flexed his muscles. "I love this song!" he exclaimed. "It makes me get stronged up!"

In the same way that my son wants to get strong muscles, he also needs a strong family. The number one reason why you might want to consider changing your career and/or the number of hours you work is because you want a family that will thrive together in good times, pull together in tough times, and look to each other for strength, love, and support. Paul wrote, "But now abide faith, hope, love, these three; but the greatest of these is love" (1 Corinthians 13:13, NKJV).

If you are concerned about your work impacting your home life, your concerns are not unusual. "Almost one in seven employed parents (14 percent) says that over the past three months, he or she often or very often has not had the energy to do things with his or her child because of the job. If one includes 'sometimes,' the number of parents feeling depleted rises to 46 percent—almost half of all employed parents."[1]

According to *Ask the Children: What America's Children Really Think About Working Parents*, "When we compare job-to-parenting spillover and parenting-to-job spillover, here's what we find:

- "Jobs are more likely to reduce our energy for parenting than children are to reduce our energy for performing our jobs...
- "Jobs are more likely to have a negative impact on our moods with our child than our children are to have negative impact on our moods at work...
- "Jobs are more likely to have a negative impact on our performance as parents than children are to have a negative impact on our performance at work...

"Jobs deplete us for parenting far more than parenting depletes us for our work."[2]

Research done through videotape analysis reflected that indeed parents bring home negative emotions from their jobs. The "researchers found that mothers are more withdrawn on days when they feel their workload is higher and the stress among coworkers is more pronounced. After these difficult days at work, the mothers initially pay less attention to their child and appear less warm and caring. So women, like men, seem to pull back after a difficult day at work."[3]

One concern of parents is that their children will experience the repercussions of their work pressures. "To what extent do children ages 13 through 18 agree that children have to grow up too fast because of the pressures of their parents' work and family life? Almost half, 48 percent, agree: 18 percent strongly and 29 percent somewhat....Although children are less likely than parents to think that children have to grow up too fast because of the pressures of their parents' work and family lives, sizable and alarming proportions of both groups feel that this is a problem: 48 percent of the children and 70.5 percent of the parents."[4]

By the numbers mentioned above, you can see that parents struggle with the balance between their work and life and with the impact it has on their children. These numbers may also be a great reminder of why you might want to change your career and/or the number of hours you work, because your family needs to come first.

Increased stress in your home life can also impact the spiritual life of your child. Paul wrote in Ephesians 6:4, "Fathers, do not provoke your children to anger, but bring them up in the discipline and instruction of the Lord" (NAS). If your children are dealing with stress and frustration that you bring home from work, this can cause stress to be a constant part of your family relationships. In addition, if the time you have with your child is limited because of work, you have less opportunity to teach and demonstrate biblical teachings in your home. Learning about God's Word from you, their parents, can have a huge effect on how a child develops his or her own relationship with Christ.

Jesus,

Your presence can bring such peace, even on the most stressful days. Please help me to remember to look to You at all times, especially when I'm worried about my family. Help me to remember to seek time with You often and to teach my children about Your gift of peace. Amen.

CHAPTER 15

What History Has Taught Me; Why I Made This Decision

> It comes down to this: you must learn how to distinguish between "need-to-have" and "want-to-have." Truly...Americans have been acculturated to want much more than they need. We basically took it for granted that we would often settle for what we needed and forgo what was not a necessity...and who missed it all in the end?
>
> —College Professor

> The trouble we are having with our children is linked directly to routine panic and the increasing isolation and detachment from you, their parents...59 percent of today's kids come home to an empty house.[1]
>
> —Dr. James Dobson

As a child, I never came home to an empty house. I was blessed with a mother who was there to welcome me home, and the security that I felt from her presence was a constant comfort, especially on days when the tragedies of girlhood problems were overwhelming. When I look back and try to imagine what my experience would have been like to come home to an empty house, it saddens me. I realize now, as a parent, how blessed I was to have a stay-at-home parent.

One benefit of having a parent at home was that she spent countless hours teaching me about God's love. This was one of my mother's greatest gifts to me. In the Bible, Moses told the children of Israel, "Repeat them again and again to your children. Talk about them when you are at home and when you are on the road, when you are going to bed and when you are getting up. Tie them to your hands and wear them on your forehead as reminders. Write them on the doorposts of your house and on your gates" (Deuteronomy 6:7-9, NLT). From biblical times we've been told to teach God's Word regularly, and being with your children often will allow you that time.

When my children are grown, I hope their memories from childhood include the comfort of sharing meals with family every day, the delight of jumping in the leaves outside on an October afternoon, and the warmth of cuddling with their parent after waking from a nap or while reading a book. My desire is to help them avoid the rush of getting ready in the morning so that we can enjoy breakfast and not get stressed out by mommy and daddy needing to leave by a certain time. I want them to remember having the occasional babysitter and time with grandparents, but most of the time being home with mom or dad. I want them to remember having mom's arms wrapped around their waists as they waved good-bye to daddy in the morning. I want them to remember peaceful and enjoyable family dinners, without their parents rushing to do errands or make dinner after a full day at the office. And I hope that those memories reassure them as they grow older that they are special and more important to me than an extra salary that we can really survive without. *My children are the riches in our family*. The changes we made were truly not a "sacrifice" because our family blessing was to be together.

According to an Ellison Research family news release, published in 2004, a study was conducted among a representative sample of 695 Protestant church ministers nationwide, asking "pastors to identify the three strongest threats to families in their own communities." From the responses given by these pastors, the researchers compiled the top five threats:[2]

1. Divorce
2. Negative influences from the media
3. Materialism
4. Absentee fathers
5. Families that lack a stay-at-home parent

In this study, 22 percent of the respondents listed families that lack a stay-at-home parent as a threat to families.[3] This is not a small number, but one that demonstrates the significance of the decisions you make for your children. It is time for us to learn from history and apply what we've learned as best as we can.

Dear Lord,

Learning from mistakes is something I've done since childhood. Forgive me for bad choices I've made, and guide me toward a life that honors You. Help me apply what I've learned from my own mistakes as well as the mistakes of others. Help me give my children the time and love that are so important for their spiritual, physical, and emotional growth. Amen.

CHAPTER 16

Survey Results: "Why Did I Leave Work or Reduce My Work Hours?"

So many people believe they need to have both parents working to maintain their lifestyle. That may be true, but do you really need that big house? Do you really need the new electronics/toys/cars? Do you really need the big vacations? I have a feeling that most young kids would rather have their parents' time than the extras. Cut down on the extras—give them yourself.

—Part-Time Doctor of Physical Therapy

Proverbs 22:6 says "Train up a child in the way he should go, and when he is old he will not depart from it" (NKJV). From the time our children are born, we should be preparing them for eternity with God the Father. Many of the lessons our children learn from us are from watching our actions. On the surveys I received from parents, they provided their reasons for leaving work or reducing their work hours. Some of the parents became stay-at-home moms and dads, others reduced their work hours so that they could be home more hours, and some started part-time businesses from home.

Below are some of their responses to the statement "The reason that I chose to leave work full-time was..."

To be able to spend time with and raise my children.

—Stay-at-Home-Mom (SAHM)

I believe it is very important to the development of my children and the well-being of my family that one of the parents be the main caretaker of our children.

—Part-Time Doctor of Physical Therapy

I felt it was extremely important for my son and future children to spend the first years of life developing and growing in their home environment, with their mom or dad as their primary caregiver.

—Part-Time Job Developer

Because I wanted to enjoy my children. Also, working stressed me out, and I found that I did not have the patience I needed after a long day at work. Now, my job is to create a nice home environment for my children and for my husband. We are all less stressed and happier for it. Life is not so rushed. We can relax and enjoy each other.

—Stay-at-Home-Mom (SAHM)

My children are my primary responsibility in life. I couldn't let someone else raise them.

—Creative Memories Consultant

I *wanted* to take care of and raise my child. I was not comfortable at all with the idea of other people raising and taking care of him for ten hours a day, five days a week. It didn't feel "right" to me.

—Senior Graphic Designer

I wanted to raise my own children.

—Teacher Who Became a SAHM

We wanted to care for our own children. My spouse is a firefighter who works twenty-four hour shifts, ten days a month, so one of us is always with them. Although we are together less, we think the trade-off is great.

—Physician Assistant

I wanted to be involved in my children's lives and enjoy their experiences with them.

—Human Resources Consultant

Because children are more important than money and possessions.

—Legal Secretary

One of the messages I received loud and clear while receiving, reading through, and analyzing the surveys was that parents felt their decisions to reduce their work hours or leave the workforce were worth every challenge they faced. Again and again they spoke of their desire to be the ones to help shape their children's confidence, security, and daily learning through being with them as much as they could.

These parents are not alone.

- "The percentage of stay-at-home moms has risen steadily since 1995, from 34 percent to 37 percent, according to the U.S. Census Bureau."[1]
- "The latest U.S. Census Bureau statistics show there are 105,000 dads who stay home primarily to take care of their children."[2]

Books, journals, and articles have been dedicated to the bantering over the issue of quality time versus quantity of time parents spend, and the results for their children. The parents who responded to my survey made it clear that they valued both, but that making the most time available for their kids was their top priority.

Dear Lord,

Help me as I "train my child up in the way he or she should go." Give me discernment and wisdom as I make decisions that impact my family, and help me to be a good role model for my child. Amen.

CHAPTER 17

From a Child's Perspective

Butch dictates a letter for his day-care provider to write to his mother:
"I wish you didn't have to work, Mommy. I wish you could stay home and take care of me. I wish I could just come to school in the morning and then go home and have lunch with you. I like to go to school, but I don't like it all day because I want to play with you sometimes."[1]

The majority of this book is written from the parents' perspective because it focuses on how to make changes for your family. However, the ultimate purpose of this book is to do what is best for your children and your family life. Because of this purpose, it is important to consider the perspective of your child.

Based on their short experience in life, children tend to focus only on their own wants and needs. Once you become a parent, however, you have to consider your children's and your own wants and needs in your decision making. Even if you have no children yet, or if you have a child on the way, your decisions will impact how he or she will approach life. Your child's life perspective will be dependent on the kind of life you provide from the very beginning.

As you are determining whether you will work outside the home full-time, part-time, or not at all, take an hour or two to look at your financial situation by using the financial sections of this book; also, consider what is truly in the best interest of your family. If you can make the choice to be with your child more by working part-time or less, *what would it mean to him or her* if you did?

Two day-care center providers, William and Wendy Dreskin, observed the impact of day-care firsthand on children. While running their day-care center, the Dreskins kept journals. One entry is below:

> Three-year-olds…often had a keen sense of what was important in *their* life. We heard Billy and Barry's mother say, "Mommy is working so we can take nice vacations and go skiing. You want to go to the snow, don't you, Barry?" Barry was not beguiled. With pain in his eyes he said quietly, "No, Mommy, we'd rather have you."[2]

In November 2007, a woman written about in a news article for the *Buffalo News* said that she found continuing in her job "extremely difficult when attempting to raise a family." Debbie Buckley, a registered nurse, said, "Mandatory overtime was a major obstacle. It was a constant struggle regarding priorities and balancing my commitment between home and work. Unfortunately, there are only 24 hours in a day, and a decision had to be made. I chose my children." Buckley "remembers missing Christmas and other holidays with her children."[3]

Buckley, like many parents, spent time considering her child's perspective when making her decision about work hours.

While thinking about your own family and your children's needs, pray for the Lord's help. Jesus expressed His love for children so clearly through His words and actions. As believers we can try to follow His lead as much as possible when making decisions for our families.

Dear Lord,

Help me to see how precious my child is in Your sight. My child looks to me for love, time, and guidance. Give me patience for my child and his/her needs, and wisdom to help me with decisions that impact my child. Please help our family keep You in the center as a constant presence in our lives, and help me to remember that You are always with us. Amen.

CHAPTER 18

"How Might My Occupation Change?"

> It is the BEST decision I've made. I learned to trust my own capabilities as a mother, wife, and business owner. I learned that God will provide what I need. At first, I struggled with balancing everything—and still do sometimes. However, I've learned systems and how to use tools to help me plan my schedule. I've also learned to be flexible enough to work around a baby with constantly changing needs. It was important to me *not* to listen to my critics who thought I wouldn't be able to make such a drastic career shift.
>
> —INDEPENDENT SALES DIRECTOR, MARY KAY COSMETICS, INC.

The following job changes are based on men and women who reduced or eliminated their work hours to be home with their children. This group of people included a mixture of parents who became full-time stay-at-home parents, started a home business, or went to part-time hours in the same or different line of work.

Occupation Before Children	Occupation After Children *(If a career is listed below, it is part-time)*
Performance Development Manager	Performance Consultant/Trainer
Accountant/Financial Manager	Job Developer
Flight Attendant	Leave of Absence Status
Performance Consultant, Human Resources	Independent Sales Consultant, Mary Kay Cosmetics, Inc.
Bank Clerk	Office Manager for Spouse's Business
Speech Therapist	Stay-at-Home Mom
Christian Education Director	Creative Memories Consultant

Senior Graphic Designer	Senior Graphic Designer
Regional Sales Manager, Telecom Industry	Stay-at-Home Mom
Human Resources Manager	Human Resources Consultant
Teacher	Teacher and Piano Teacher
Training Manager	Training Consultant
Doctor of Physical Therapy	Doctor of Physical Therapy
Physical Therapist	Physical Therapist
Physician Assistant	Physician Assistant
Day-care Worker/Assistant Director	Preschool Teacher
Office Manager	Stay-at-Home Mom
Technical Support for Library	Stay-at-Home Mom
Trainer	Trainer

The survey respondents demonstrated creativity in how they changed their careers in order to be home with their children more. Some of them swapped time with their spouse, going to part-time evening or weekend hours. Others started new businesses that they ran from their homes. And others took time off altogether while their children were young and then returned to the workforce once their children were in school.

Not every career can be done part-time or done through a home business. I was in a career where I started a business I could run from a home office. I scheduled work with clients only when Grandma or an occasional babysitter was available, and I often did design work when my husband was home or my children were napping. That arrangement worked for me, but it won't work in every situation. I also realize that not everyone even wants to start their own business! The goal of this book is to give you creative ideas that others have tried so that you can begin to build on your own strengths, backgrounds, and resources.

> Look, for example, at the Stanford class of '81. Fifty-seven percent of mothers in that class spent at least a year at home caring for their infant children in the first decade after graduation. One out of four have stayed home three or more years. Look at Harvard Business School. A survey of women from the classes of 1981, 1985, and 1991 found that only 38 percent were working full time. Look at professional women in surveys across the board. Between one-quarter and one-third are out of the work force, depending on the study and the profession. Look at the United States

> Census, which shows that the number of children being cared for by stay-at-home moms has increased nearly 13 percent in less than a decade. At the same time, the percentage of new mothers who go back to work fell from 59 percent in 1998 to 55 percent in 2000.
>
> Look, too, at the mothers who have not left completely but have scaled down or redefined their roles in the crucial career-building years (25 to 44). Two-thirds of those mothers work fewer than 40 hours a week—in other words, part-time. Only 5 percent work 50 or more hours weekly. Women leave the workplace to strike out on their own at equally telling rates; the number of businesses owned or co-owned by women jumped 11 percent since 1997, nearly twice the rate of businesses in general.[1]

Clearly, parents have been making changes in their work situations, and they will continue to do so. After considering what other parents have tried, you can now begin to explore what changes might be possible for your own family.

Dear Lord,

Thank You for the willingness of other parents to share their ideas in this book. The comfort I get from knowing other parents struggle as I do, and yet persevere with Your support, helps me. Please watch over our family as we consider the ideas others have tried, and help us to balance our time for the good of our family. Amen.

CHAPTER 19

Quantity versus Quality

> I learned very quickly that you can never get the time back that you miss away from your children. I didn't like hearing that they took a first step or said a new word and that I missed it. They grow up so fast. You really only have five years and then off they go to school—it's not that long. One can always return to a career in five years.
>
> —Parish Ministry Consultant

Back to the eternal debate that has been heard around the world: *quality time versus quantity of time with children.*

> When we ask the children, we find that the *amount* of time they report spending with their mothers and their fathers certainly does affect how they see their parents. But so do the content and quality of time: the activities they engage in with their parents, whether or not the time they have together is frantic or calm, and whether they believe that their parents are really focusing on them when they are together. So whereas the national discussion on work and parenting has polarized the issue of time into quality versus quantity, our data indicate that *both* quality *and* quantity matter.[1]

I feel that quality time will always be cherished by your children. It is those moments when your eyes and ears are totally on them. "Can you read this to me, Daddy?" asks your daughter. "Mom, watch me do this!" says your son. Reading her that story and praising his newest accomplishment are some ways of providing quality time for our children. We are giving our undivided attention. Focused attention is the best gift. "As each one has received a special gift, employ it in serving one another as good stewards of the manifold grace of God" (1 Peter 4:10, NAS). Quality time is priceless—and necessary—for healthy bonding with children.

Quantity of time is the *amount of time* we spend with our children. This is also important. We don't even have to speak during these times, those quiet moments when we are in the same room, when we are riding in the same car, when we are listening to the same song. Simply being together, being there, builds security in our children.

I've read countless articles that debate that quantity of time doesn't matter as long as you have lots of quality time with your child. Although I agree that quality time is important, from my own experience I've found that when you have a lot of *quantity time*, it provides ideal amounts of time for *quality*.

When I have the daytime hours to do the grocery shopping, laundry, and doctor's visits, it makes it much easier to provide quality time during the day and in the evening when the home tasks are done. It also makes it possible for my husband to have much more quality time when he gets home. He is not worrying about throwing together dinner, cleaning up the living room, and getting clean socks through the laundry, but instead he has time to enjoy our children.

> Because parents are so activity-oriented, they tend to rate time spent "doing things" with their children as constructive and ignore the rest. "What with cleaning, shopping, and cooking I really only played with him an hour a day anyway." What that mother does not realize is that to a young child her presence, even in another room, makes a big difference. The experience of building a block tower in the living room knowing Mommy's in the kitchen *is* very different from the experience of building a block tower in the house alone or with a sitter in the next room. It may feel the same to the mother to cook dinner with her child out of the house or playing in the next room, but to her child the ability to touch base makes all the difference in the world. When children feel they are being cared for by that special person, the feeling determines the quality of their experience no matter what activity they are engaged in.[2]

I feel that if I were working every day, evenings would be our time to catch up on the housework and errands rather than our time to spend as a family enjoying each other, reading, playing, and bonding. Yes, you *can* bond while you empty the dishwasher together, but it is hard to bond with an eighteen-month-old over the dishwasher. Time playing on the floor is much more his or her style, and having the time to do that means the world to a child. Sometimes it is OK to have dirty dishes in the sink for an evening.

One piece of housework or an errand can be a bonding experience, but when you are trying to jam all of your errands and household duties into the few hours of the evening, the opportunity to really enjoy the errand together can be tainted by the need to rush through many things and get everything done. Some families actually schedule household chores, such as laundry on Monday, collecting garbage on Wednesday, etc., so that they don't get overwhelmed by trying to do too much in one day.

> Again and again—in fact, *in all but one* of the analyses conducted to address this issue—we found that the quantity of time with mothers and fathers does matter a great deal. Children who spend more time with their mothers and fathers on workdays and nonworkdays grade their parents higher, feel their parents are more successful at managing work and family responsibilities, and see their parents as putting their families first.
>
> For the most part, these statistics are quite striking. For example, far more children who spend 6 hours a day with their mothers on workdays give the mothers an A for making them feel important and loved (83 percent) than those who spend less than 1 hour with their mothers on workdays (62 percent).[3]

Time spent with our children is important. The next chapter helps you to consider how you spend your time daily.

Dear Lord,

This is a tough one! Sometimes I feel like I just can't give my children enough of my time. I know that spending time with me is important to my children, but sometimes I get so distracted by tasks I need to do that I don't slow down enough to give my children what they need. Please help me to be patient with myself and with my children. Help me to "slow down" the pace. Remind me to listen to my children, to hold them, and to spend time with them. Amen.

CHAPTER 20

Family Time

I delight to do Your will, O my God.

—Psalm 40:8, NAS

Sample of hours spent daily

Where Can Your Family Time Go?					
Typical hours when both parents are working			**Typical hours when one parent is working** ***(example based on father working)***		
Hours spent daily	**Mom**	**Dad**	**Hours spent daily**	**Mom**	**Dad**
With family	4	4	With family	13	4
At or traveling to work	9	9	At or traveling to work	0	9
Extracurricular or household duties	2	2	Extracurricular or household duties	2	2
Sleep or getting ready in morning	9	9	Sleep or getting ready in morning	9	9
TOTAL FAMILY HOURS: 8			TOTAL FAMILY HOURS: 17		
TOTAL WORK HOURS: 18			TOTAL WORK HOURS: 9		

So, where can family time go? Based on the typical workday hours, the chart above shows how time availability can change based on both parents working versus one parent working full-time. For this example, I based the hours first on both parents working and then on just the father working. Although the parents I surveyed did not always have the mother at home while the father was in the workforce, it was more often the case. However, if you are the mom and will be the one in the workforce while your husband is home with the kids, you can still use the same basic numbers to consider your family time.

Perhaps you are considering part-time hours, and in that case the amount of hours on this chart would be somewhere in the middle. The point of this is to encourage you to consider where your time is going and how that fits into your priorities as a family.

Dear Lord,

Thank You for being there every day, every moment. Please help me to make decisions that are best for my children. Thank You for Your many blessings, especially Your gift of time with my family. Amen.

Part 4

MORE TO CONSIDER

CHAPTER 21

Who Takes Care of the Children?

Let all that you do be done in love.

—1 Corinthians 16:14, NAS

In my survey, I asked parents, "Who helps take care of your children when you are working part-time hours or are just out for other reasons." They listed family members and babysitters most often. Some of the parents needed help when they were working part-time hours, and others simply needed a night out with their spouse. Below are the percentages showing their responses:

AUTHOR'S NOTE: The total percentage below is more than 100 percent because often more than one answer fit for each survey respondent. For example, a survey respondent would often check both answers under grandparents and babysitter.

- 43 percent grandparents
- 38 percent spouse
- 9 percent other family members besides grandparents
- 5 percent friends

If you decide to reduce your work hours, you may have to rethink your child-care situation. For example, some day-care centers require that you utilize their services a certain amount of days or hours in order to place your child there. In my case, I was unable to schedule work projects on Wednesdays and some Tuesdays because of my child-care providers' schedules. I was able to work my projects around the other days. Whatever your situation, you should think this over before making any announcements about changing your work situation. That will help you ease into the transition of working full-time to part-time or no hours.

Also keep in mind that you will need to keep the lines of communication open with your children regarding their child care:

> Children, too, can be reluctant to tell us that child care isn't working. I was in a child's bedroom in Los Angeles, sitting at the foot of her bed, talking with her and her sister, when one of the girls confided in me that they didn't like their babysitter. I asked them whether they had told their mother or father about this, and they both chorused, "No." "Why not?" I asked. "Because the next one might be worse." Likewise, a ten-year-old boy told me that he hadn't told his parents about some of the things his family child care provider had done (such as leaving him in charge of the babies while she ran errands) because he didn't want to upset his parents. They were so proud that they were using a "good" child care provider.[1]

If you decide to leave the work force and be a full-time stay-at-home parent, you will still need some time away from the home to do special errands or spend time with your spouse. In this case it is also important to consider the best way to address your child-care needs.

Dear Lord,

Thank You for the caretakers in the lives of our children. Thank You for the family and friends who love them and teach them to honor You. Help us to remember to thank them often. Amen.

CHAPTER 22

What Will You Encounter When You Want to *Increase* Your Work Hours?

> My husband and I are thankful we were able to raise our children with me at home during those early years. Now I am back to work doing what I love, and the long-range positive influences on my children can still be seen today.
>
> —Teacher and Former Stay-at-Home Mom

While researching this book, I surveyed people who decided to return to work once their children were school age. These parents had put their career on hold for a time or had reduced their career "push" while they had young families. The survey questions focused on returning to work in some form, and parents had a lot to say, both good and bad. If you are concerned about your reentry back into the workforce or about increasing your work hours, their insights may interest you.

Positive Responses to Returning to Work

- "Interacting with colleagues"
- "Expanding my work experiences"
- "Increasing income"
- "Working in a job that I enjoy with people who are fun to work with and learn from"
- "It gave me the opportunity to reconnect with my peers and to have adult interaction and socialization."

- "I work with a bunch of other moms, so I've been getting good advice on child raising from them."
- "Having conversation and social time with other adults"
- "Financial independence"
- "Enjoying the feeling of being a part of something other than my typical home duties. It is nice to have 'break' from being 'mommy' and experience being 'me' again."
- "It forced me to let my spouse be a true 'co-parent.' It was very difficult for me to let go and share that role, but it was empowering for him, and he has continued to really be an equal parent."
- "Helped the kids transition from constantly needing my attention to becoming more independent and needing attention in a different way—by just being there, talking and guiding them."

Challenges at the End of the Day

- "Not being home to welcome our children and hear about their day when they get off the bus at the end of the school day."
- "Not enough time and too exhausted physically to enjoy time with family."
- "The most challenging part of my day is to come home at night after a long day of work and my spouse is gone (he works a twenty-four-hour shift) to two tired, over-sugared kids who expect the complete and undivided attention they have enjoyed the entire day with their grandmother."

Challenges at Certain Times of Year

- "Not being with our children on their holidays, vacation days, summer vacation, and when they are sick"
- "When our baby has been sick, it's been really hard to juggle work and take time off for him."

Child-Care Challenges

Child care continues to be a challenge for some. As one parent put it, "The most challenging part is finding reliable child care I can trust. I am able to schedule most of my hours when my husband is home."

The Continuing Challenge of Balance

Balance is a theme mentioned often by parents returning to more work hours. Here are some challenges:

- "Balancing work and home commitments"
- "Balancing and GUILT. I feel fortunate to be able to work AND be a mother AND be a wife AND a runner AND... However, the difficulty is doing anything well—but I do a lot. Sleep is what gets shortchanged. My goal is six hours a night, and that is not common."
- "Finding the balance between work and home life and managing all of the tasks involved with both"
- "Helping my kids transition from me being home full-time"

Concern about balance between work and home "is not confined to North America. A new study by the European Foundation for the Improvement of Living and Working Conditions contends that employees working in Northern Europe enjoy better work/life balance than those in Southern Europe. According to Reuters, the study asked 21,000 companies operating in the European Union to answer questions about flextime, family leave, retirement and the ability of employees to shift from full-time to part-time duties. The results indicate a clear north-south divide, with companies in the Mediterranean having a more rigid working structure."[1] Whether in North America or other locations, families are facing the issue of balance.

Next, I asked parents, "If you could go back in time, what would you tell yourself about returning to work or increasing your work hours? What would you anticipate or try to do differently?" Replies included:

- "Make greater sacrifices to find a way to get by on less income."
- "Be ready for work before the kids get up. Have that casual feeling in the morning that doesn't seem like you are being

rushed to find the keys, make the lunches, lay out the clothes. Get up earlier and sit on the floor and play trucks until you peacefully walk out the door on time with a hug and a kiss and no panic or rush."

- "Be realistic that things cannot be perfect—the floor cannot be cleaned every night; laundry will get backed up; we cannot eat regular family dinners; it is OK not to be a good cook; etc."
- "You cannot be simultaneously great on the career track and mommy track—both have to give if you do both. No one wants to say this, but it is true."
- "I may tell myself to anticipate having to juggle my schedule when my child gets sick."
- "I would tell myself not to be so hard on myself and to allow for down time without feeling guilty that I should be doing something for either work or home and that it is OK to take some time for me."

Who and What Made the Transition Back to Work Easier

- "My husband, who is supportive and helpful."
- "My spouse. He comes home in the morning and takes over seamlessly and full of energy. Rarely did I see any screaming, pleading, or crying at the door. They are always happy to see him, and they hardly fret that I am leaving."
- "Multitalented and supportive husband with a flexible work schedule."
- "I am blessed with great babysitters and a wonderful family."
- "My husband was/is very helpful in helping keep the balance by offering assistance on both home and work tasks as well as keeping me focused on what is important."
- "My parents."

- "My husband meets the kids when they get home each day from school. He also helps with cooking supper and folding laundry. Our children help with household chores."
- "We carpool, which helps. My husband takes on extra chores on the days we both work."
- "My husband is very supportive in many ways. He helps with household chores without being asked."
- "Our neighbors have been a huge source of help for those little emergencies and long days with the toddler when you thought you would go insane. One early-morning work meeting or a late afternoon at work, and you just need one hour of help. My neighbors made all the difference."
- "Swapping babysitting for a couple of hours once a month with our neighbors, so my spouse and I could have dinner together."

Parents also were thankful for technology, flexible companies to work for, and after-school programs.

Technology and Tools

- "Cell phones! We can communicate so much easier and more often. When I have to be away from the kids, I don't worry about them because I know they can reach me anytime."
- "My spouse never had a phone until we had kids; then it was a must. We had to know each other's whereabouts all the time from the day our first child was born so we could plan our day."
- "Monitors allowed me to go to the neighbors backyard after bedtime and have some semblance of a social life."
- "I work for a technology company, so we have all the latest and greatest tools to allow work from home."
- "We use a family calendar on the refrigerator to help with communication between me and my husband. This way he knows what to expect for the upcoming month."

- "We would leave a tape player on our counter, so that when our kids came home from school I could record the conversation about our day. Later, my spouse could hear the everyday excitement right from their mouths if he had a late shift or was traveling. My husband could play it for me as well if I was working late."

Understanding Organizations

- "My firm where I work is flexible when it comes to shifting hours or making up time missed for sick days, doctor appointments, baseball games, etc."
- "Being able to conduct most of my work from home was very helpful for me and my family."
- "Flexible work hours. My boss truly understands because he has children the exact same age as mine!"
- "My boss, who is very family friendly and allows me to have the freedom to put my family concerns first. My co-workers also, who are very family oriented—so they have dealt with some of the same balancing issues I am now facing."

School Programs

- "After-school care providers."
- "Our elementary school has an excellent, affordable after-school program on the premises, which I am hoping will make the transition easier for my boys when school starts."

Parents then responded to these questions: "Do you feel that your transition was a successful one? How would you define success in this case?" In general, the respondents felt that they had been successful. They defined success by how their children were reacting and by how their children are growing up. They also defined success by their own feelings of fulfillment or their family's sense of balance.

I asked these parents: "What was the best decision you've ever made about balancing work and your family? What was the worst decision you've ever made about balancing work and your family?" Below is some of their responses.

Best Decision I've Made

- "Staying home with our children when they were preschool age."
- "To gradually increase my work hours based on the age of my children and reducing my hours when they proved to be over the top."
- "Having babysitters come to the house. Picking and dropping the children off is very stressful."
- "Working for a company that understands balance."
- "Only going back part-time. It would be very difficult to work full-time and still have enough time for my family."
- "To yield to God's plan for our family and to be faithful to His plan. I learned early that I could not do this on my own."
- "Listening to and getting advice from Dr. Dobson and *Focus on the Family!* I know this doesn't seem related to the topic, but it actually is. They have helped me balance work and family and keep things in the proper perspective. I've listened for over twenty years and consider them my best source of encouragement, support, and just plain great ideas!"

Worst Decision I've Made

- "No 'worst,' but many learning experiences—worked very late and did not see children all day; missing some performances, etc."
- "In the beginning and at times when things become overwhelming, not doing a good job balancing the priorities."
- "Trying to 'do it all' by not communicating to my husband when I needed help or a break." (Look back at the "Keeping Your Sanity" chapter under the "check-in" section for ideas that relate to this.)
- "Working full-time."

- "Relying on family to care for my kids (ironically the best and worst decision). It is a big source of conflict for me and my spouse, who needs to mediate between his family and me if we ever disagree."

Lessons From Life

At the end of the survey, I asked parents to share any real-life experiences or family stories that they thought could demonstrate the challenge of balancing work and family. Here were some of their responses:

- "I will never forget Monday through Friday mornings twenty years ago when my girls were very young. My husband was in school full-time and therefore I had to work full-time. While I was rushing around trying to get ready, my youngest daughter, usually crying, would be clinging to my leg. It was the most frustrating time of my life. I didn't want to have to go to work full-time, but I had to."
- "My five-year-old daughter asks, 'What have you done at work today, Mom?' every night. I think that is important as a female role model. My son, also five, does not leave my side when I work late the day before. He asks to come to work and asks me not to go."

Tools and Tips to Help You Succeed

If you do decide to go back to more work hours, here are some additional points to keep in mind: check your résumé, your contacts, your options for job searching, your wardrobe, and your childcare options.

Your résumé

If you don't already have a résumé, you should create one. To get ideas for how to create a résumé, you can either use a template from your computer, do research on the Internet on how to create a résumé, or hire a business writing advisor to help you create one. You should also create a cover letter to send with your résumé for job applications.

This is a critical time regarding updating your résumé. You'll want to demonstrate how you "stayed in the business" as much as possible. Updating your résumé can be a daunting task for anyone, but it can be especially frustrating if you feel like you don't have enough experience to put on your résumé. Some things to remember include:

1. Take advantage of résumé services; there are organizations who perform résumé editing services. I do that as part of my business, and there are a lot of recruiting agencies and other agencies that can provide this type of assistance. Research organizations like this in your area and get their advice.
2. Include any volunteer work or leadership work on your résumé. You don't have to be paid to do something for it to go on your résumé. Did you lead or work on a fund-raising effort for your child's school or oversee a sport's team? Did you organize field trips and other school or church activities? Did you lead a book club? Think of the ways you have made a contribution and add them to your résumé.
3. Write a solid cover letter and get feedback on it. Most employers expect a cover letter with a résumé. Often those who provide résumé services also give advice on cover letters.

Chances are that you have some good experiences that you can put on your resume. "Contemporary woman are different because they usually have had some kind of work experience, even when careers are put aside to focus on a family."[2]

Your potential work contacts

You knew people in the workforce before children, and you still do. Do some networking. Let people you know personally know that you are interested in working outside the home. Sometimes getting the perfect job is just a matter of knowing the right person at the right time. Share that you are searching for a particular kind of job, and you might find some good connections through people you already know and trust.

Your options for job searching

Job searching can be done through many mediums: searching the local newspaper, job ads on bulletin boards at restaurants, and other ways. But the one area where you have to be up to speed is job searching on the Internet. If you haven't become familiar with the Internet, this is the time to learn. Take a course, or get training from a friend so that you are comfortable searching the Web and looking for employment. In the process, you'll learn a skill you can apply at many jobs. Knowing how to navigate through an Internet Web site is important to a lot of jobs. "To land such jobs women must figure out how to search Internet lists, post résumés electronically and fill out applications at store computer kiosks."[3]

Your wardrobe

According to an article in *The Buffalo News*, Everywoman Opportunity Center said, "A lot of women don't spend money on the kind of dress clothes they need to win a job in an interview. So a closet at the center has good work outfits people can take to get started."[4] Perhaps there is an organization like Everywoman Opportunity Center in your area that will allow you to borrow interview clothes.

First impressions are critical when trying to get a job. Be sure that you are dressed appropriately for a job interview, or you'll already have one strike against you before you've even said a word.

Your child-care options

Be sure to research your child-care options carefully. You want to have a solid idea of what your options are before you have a job interview. The last thing you want to do is be distracted during an interview because you haven't planned how you'll manage child care. You also want to be clear about what hours you can work before you start to search. If you have no child-care options for daytime, then you might have to search for jobs that have evening hours only, and so on.

There will be different challenges for all, depending on your own family structure and work structure. Whatever the outcome, you are a strong contributor, as indicated below by the advice Abigail Van Buren gave to a question posed to her in 2006:

> ***Dear Abby:*** I need your help with something. My 16-year-old grandson seems to think that all his mother does is stay at home. He conveniently "forgets" that she is a housekeeper, gardener, cook, teacher, nurse, driver and mediator. Could you please print a breakdown of what a stay-at-home wife should be paid? I would love to have a list so I can pass the "bill" on to him.
>
> VIVIAN IN COLONIAL BEACH, VA.

Dear Vivian: According to the Census Bureau figures for 2004—which are the most recent—there are 36.7 million mothers of minor children in the United States. About one-third of them, 10.8 million, are stay-at-home moms.

According to an article penned by Al Neuharth, the founder of *USA Today*, in its May 11, 2006, edition, "Salary.com compensation experts estimate that stay-at-home moms work an average of 91.6 hours a week." That's more than double the number of hours the average office worker puts in. He went on to say, "That should be worth $134,121 annually."

He quoted compensation analysts as figuring the lowest-paying parts of a mother's job are "housekeeper, laundry machine operator and janitor. Higher-paying categories include computer operator, facilities manager, psychologist, and CEO." With a 91.6-hour work week, 52 weeks a year, it works out to be $28.16 an hour.

It should go without saying that a mother's love is priceless, so tell that grandson of yours that $28.16 an hour is a real bargain.

CHAPTER 23

Resources List

The resources listed in this section include books and Web sites that cover topics that are important for families. The topics include financial management, challenges with children, home businesses, ideas for stay-at-home parents, and more.

Books

Bach, David. *Smart Women Finish Rich*. N.p.: Broadway Books, 1999, 2002.

Calloway, Phil. *I Used to Have Answers, Now I Have Kids*. Eugene, OR: Harvest House Publishers, 2000.

Dacyczyn, Amy. *The Complete Tightwad Gazette*. New York: Villard Books, a division of Random House, Inc., 1998.

Dobson, James. *Bringing Up Boys: Practical Advice and Encouragement for Those Shaping the Next Generation of Men*. Wheaton, IL: Tyndale House Publishers, 2001.

Leman, Dr. Kevin. *Making Children Mind Without Losing Yours*. Grand Rapids, MI: Fleming H. Revell, a division of Baker Book House Co., 2000.

McCoy, Jonni. *Miserly Moms: Living on One Income in a Two-Income Economy*, 3rd edition. Minneapolis, MN: Bethany House Publishers, 2001.

Partow, Donna. *Homemade Business*. N.p.: Focus on the Family Publishing, 1992.

Quigley, Mary W. and Loretta E. Kaufman. *Going Back to Work: A Survival Guide for Comeback Moms*. Griffin, NY: St. Martin's, 2004.

Schlessinger, Laura. *Parenthood by Proxy: Don't Have Them If You Won't Raise Them*. New York: Cliff Street Books, an Imprint of HarperCollins Publishers, 2000.

Web Sites

Web Site Address	Information provided
www.ditchthe.com	Cathi Brese Doebler's website, including a link to her blog, which mainly focuses on parenting.
www.mommysavers.com/work_from_home_ideas.htm	Work at home ideas and links to additional articles on the subject
www.drlaura.com/sah/money.html	Articles on how to start making money at home
www.Coolsavings.com	Online coupons available
www.Valupage.com	Online coupons available
www.daveramsey.com	Home page for the host of *The Dave Ramsey show* and author of *The Total Money Makeover*
www.drlaura.com/sah/budget.html	Articles on how to save money
www.notjustbeans.com	Frugal cookbook: *50 Years of Frugal Family Favorites* (has over 540 recipes and 400 tips)
www.Bankrate.com	Site where you can check mortgage rates as well as credit card rates
www.cardweb.com	Site where you can find lower-interest credit card rates with no annual fee
www.salary.com	Site that has salary survey information to help you determine if your spouse is underpaid
www.drlaura.com/sah/sahd.html	Encouragement for stay-at-home dads
www.mommysavers.com/welcome-home/stay_at_home_moms.htm	Encouraging stories from moms who have stayed home before
www.AtHomeMother.com	Site for National Association of At Home Mothers
www.momslikeme.com	A networking Web site for moms

www.homebodies.org	Created by Cheryl Gochnauer, a stay-at-home mom
www.drlaura.com/sah/sahm.html?mode=view&tile=1&id=722	Online resources for stay-at-home parents, such as national associations, nonprofit organizations, and money-saving ideas
www.epicforchildren.org	Parenting workshops and programs
www.familiesandwork.org	Families and Work Institute

CHAPTER 24

Final Advice and Thoughts

At the end of the survey, respondents who had reduced their work hours or who had become stay-at home parents were asked for any final advice they would like to share with other parents. Some of their responses have been used at the beginnings of chapters throughout this book, and many others are below:

> We only live once. The days and years fly by, especially those days of childhood. No job would be worth missing those days if you can possibly find a way to be the major caretaker for your children. On the other hand, if there is no feasible way to manage without your salary, you do what is best for your family situation and enjoy each moment you do have with your children.
>
> —Teacher Who Used To Be a SAHM

> It is impossible to do it all. You think you will have so much time to do things when you are at home all day with your child, but is just isn't so. Babies are a lot of work and take a lot of energy out of you. Sleep when you can, and don't feel guilty about not getting everything done. Set your goals small in the beginning as you adjust.
>
> —Flight Attendant (Leave of Absence Status)

> Since I have older and younger children, I think it has helped the ones I stayed home with be more secure than the ones who had day care while I worked.
>
> —Stay-at-Home Mom

> I actually do believe that parenting is a full-time job, and current societal attitudes give that short shrift. Even the big "family values" political types

currently in power would never think of finding a way to value the work of a woman in the home. If it were valued as part of our economy (e.g., social security credits), maybe so many moms wouldn't have to work after all.

—College Professor

If at all possible, spend the preschool years at home with your children and put work on "hold." Even though it may seem impossible, do whatever it takes to make it possible. Those years slip by so quickly and can never be replaced...preschool children need to know that they are more important than any job or anything that can be purchased because of a job.

—Legal Assistant

Do it. In the long run, it is much more rewarding than acquisition of those "things" people insist on the dual income to buy: a bigger, showy house; two cars; electronic gizmos up the wazoo; faux designer clothes; costly lessons for the kiddies. A healthy, happy, well-adjusted family is, as MasterCard would say, "priceless." There are also a countless number of ways to satisfy professional interests in the volunteer sector, especially in organizations that directly benefit your children and family, like Scouting, schools, etc.

—College Professor

It is a *totally* worthwhile investment. No job could pay me enough to add the stress of packing them up and dropping them off to be raised by anyone other than me (and their dad).

—Creative Memories Consultant

I am one of the very lucky few who can work from home. I never thought my employer would agree to the situation, but I ASKED about it, and it worked in my favor. I would advise anyone who is thinking about reducing their hours to think about their ideal situation and talk to their employer about it. They may be pleasantly surprised, as I was.

—Senior Graphic Designer

Even on my worst day, I don't regret my decision. I can't imagine not being with them.

—Stay-at-Home Mom

Please try to stay at home and work part-time (if you need to work). The children are little for a short time; enjoy them as much as you can. They grow up way too fast and are big before you know it. You cannot bring back time!

—Part-Time Physical Therapist

> I don't regret giving up some material things so I could be with them. Material things come and go, but children's lives are so precious.
>
> —Office Manager for Husband's Business

> My best advice would be to trust yourself and to trust God. Learn the personal and technical skills it takes, and use the resources you have available to you. Realize that you cannot turn back the hands of time; you must do what is in your heart now so you won't regret your decision later. I see a shift in our world; more women and men are realizing the importance of being back at home. This world offers us opportunities to work from home and have it all! We must make the decision. Know that it will not always be easy, but it is certainly worth it!
>
> —Independent Sales Director, Mary Kay Cosmetics, Inc.

Although I was not a survey respondent, I could certainly relate to the men and women who filled out the surveys. I had made similar choices and felt blessed to have made those choices. I knew in my heart that I could not make the whole world change for the better, but I could make a difference in the lives of my own children. The story below really brings that home as well…

> One day a man was walking along the beach when he noticed a figure in the distance. As he got closer, he realized the figure was that of a boy picking something up and gently throwing it into the ocean. Approaching the boy, he asked, "What are you doing?"
>
> The youth replied, "Throwing starfish in the ocean. The sun is up and the tide is going out. If I don't throw them in, they'll die."
>
> "Son," the man said, "don't you realize there are miles and miles and miles of beach and hundreds of starfish? You can't possibly make a difference!"
>
> After listening politely, the boy bent down, picked up another starfish, and threw it into the surf. Then, smiling at the man, he said, "I made a difference for that one."[1]

You have the potential to make the difference for your child. The action plan on the next page is your first step on your road to focusing on what is truly important, your family.

CHAPTER 25

My Action Plan

Below is an action plan template for you to use for setting your family goals. For a complete action plan tool with a step-by-step process, you can purchase the "Ditch the Joneses, Discover Your Family Workbook" at: www.ditchthe.com

Whether you have baby number one on the way, in diapers, or already in school, you can make an impact on your child through your parenting and family decisions. Take some time to discuss your goals with your family and to put together an action plan.

I plan to do the following...

(Look back at the main chapters in this book and consider how you can make adjustments for your family's benefit.)

____

____

____

____

For financial security planning...

Complete the three worksheets found earlier in this book and discuss them with your spouse:

- Can You Afford to Work?
- Determining Your Budget
- Cost Savings Ideas

Then set goals together to plan for your financial security:

To keep in touch...

I will do the following to nurture adult relationships in my life:

To keep my sanity...

I will do the following to remain focused on my family as a priority:

Dear Lord,

Be with me constantly to guide my every step. Watch over my family and help me to make good decisions for them. Thank You for Your love and Your listening ear. You are my comfort and friend. Amen.

Notes

Chapter 1
Why Did You Pick This Book Off the Shelf?

1. Joanne Watson, "Quality of Life: One Income Beats Two," http://www.sheknows.com/articles/parenting/mom/624-Quality-of-life-One-income-beats-two.htmf (accessed October 6, 2008).

2. James Dobson, *Bringing Up Boys: Practical Advice and Encouragement for Those Shaping the Next Generation of Men* (Wheaton, IL: Tyndale House Publishers, Inc., 2001), 108.

Chapter 2
Financial Decisions Are Hard; You Are Not Alone!

1. Dobson, *Bringing Up Boys*, 107–108.

Chapter 3
Plan *Before* You Start a Family

1. David Bach, *Smart Women Finish Rich: 9 Steps to Achieving Financial Security and Funding Your Dreams* (n.p.: Broadway Books, 1999, 2002), 97.

2. Ibid., 98.

3. Ibid.

Chapter 4
Can You Afford to Work?

1. Robin McClure, "Cost of Daycare: Where You Live, Quality, and Age of Kids Can Vary Rates," About.com, 2008. "Costs for typical care still range from about $100 to $400 a week for full-time care. Infant care, in part due to a lower staff-child ratio and more hands-on nurturing and care required, adds an additional $25 to $100 to that total. Additional expenses can include supply fees (which may be assessed monthly, quarterly or bi-annually), laundry or diaper assessments, and even staff development/training charges. Some centers provide internet viewing for parents (where parents can log-in to a protected website and observe their child's activities at daycare), often for an additional charge. At daycare centers, working parents may find that they still must pay their regular tuition/fees even when the center is closed for certain holidays, which means back-up care must be obtained."

2. U.S. Census Bureau, "American Community Survey (ACS)," press release, August 26, 2008, stating: "Earnings: Connecticut, New Jersey, Maryland, Massachusetts, New Hampshire and Alaska had median earnings above $50,000 for men who worked full time, year-round in the 2007 ACS. No state had median earnings for women above $50,000, but the District of Columbia, Maryland, New Jersey, Massachusetts and Connecticut had median earnings for women who worked full time, year-round above $40,000."

Data research for the ACS survey explanation: The estimates in the report *Income, Poverty, and Health Insurance Coverage in the United States: 2007* are from the 2008 Annual Social and Economic Supplement (ASEC) of the Current Population Survey (CPS). The U.S. Census Bureau conducts the ASEC over a three-month period, in February, March, and April, with most data collection occurring in the month of March. The ASEC uses two sets of questions, the basic CPS and a set of supplemental questions. The CPS, sponsored jointly by the Census Bureau and the U.S. Bureau of Labor Statistics, is the country's primary source of labor force statistics for the entire population. The Census Bureau and the Bureau of Labor Statistics also jointly sponsor the ASEC.

Also, U.S. Census Bureau Fact Sheet, "2006 American Community Survey Data Profile Highlights." "Mean travel time *to work* in minutes (workers 16 years and over) is 25 minutes."

Chapter 7
Ways to Save Money

1. Kristen Davis, "Can You Afford to Quit Work?" *Parents*, April 2005.

Chapter 8
The Impact of Changes in the Business World

1. Lisa Belkin, "The Opt-Out Revolution," *New York Times*, October 26, 2003, 8.

2. Ibid., 11.

3. Don S. Browning et al., *From Culture Wars to Common Ground: Religion and the American Family Debate* (n.p.: Westminster John Knox Press, 1997), 317.

4. Ibid., 328.

5. Siobhan Smith, "Professional Women Embarking Upon Motherhood in their 30's—Perceptual Changes in Success and Goals," unpublished college thesis, 29.

Chapter 10
Keeping in Touch

1. Davis, "Can You Afford to Quit Work?"

Chapter 11
Keeping *Your* Sanity

1. Gina Roberts-Grey, "Starting Over: Making the Transition from Working to Staying Home," *Western New York Family Magazine*, November 2005, 14.
2. Ibid.
3. Davis, "Can You Afford to Quit Work?"
4. Dobson, *Bringing Up Boys*, 106.
5. Belkin, "The Opt-Out Revolution,"
6. Roberts-Grey, "Starting Over: Making the Transition from Working to Staying Home."

Chapter 12
Maintaining *Family* Sanity

1. Ellen Galinsky, *Ask the Children: What America's Children Really Think About Working Parents* (New York: William Morrow and Company, Inc., 1999), 87.
2. Dobson, *Bringing Up Boys*, 103.

Chapter 13
Assumptions We Face

1. Dobson, *Bringing Up Boys*, 106.
2. Davis, "Can You Afford to Quit Work?"
3. Belkin, "The Opt-Out Revolution," 3.
4. Galinsky, *Ask the Children*, "Introduction."
5. Ibid., 49.
6. Ibid., 29.
7. Ibid., 56.
8. Wendy Dreskin and William Dreskin, *The Day Care Decision: What's Best for You and Your Child* (n.p.: M. Evans and Company, Inc., 1983), 34.
9. Ibid., 43, 50.
10. Smith, "Professional Women Embarking Upon Motherhood in their 30's—Perceptual Changes in Success and Goals," 8.

Chapter 14
The Reason for the Change

1. Galinsky, *Ask the Children*, 184.
2. Ibid., 197.
3. Ibid., 174.
4. Ibid., 270–271.

Chapter 15
What History Has Taught Me; Why I Made This Decision

1. Dobson, *Bringing Up Boys*, 107.

2. Ellison Research, "Protestant Clergy Name Divorce, Negative Influences From the Media, and Materialism as the Three Greatest Threats to Families in Their Community," *Facts & Trends*, November/December 2004, http://www.ellisonresearch.com/erps%20ii/release_13_family.htm (accessed October 6, 2008). The sample of 695 Protestant ministers included only those who are actively leading churches. The study's total sample is accurate to within ±3.6 percentage points at the 95 percent confidence level with a 50 percent response distribution. The study was conducted in all 50 states, using a representative sample of pastors from all Protestant denominations. Respondents' geography, church size, and denomination were carefully tracked to ensure appropriate representation and accuracy.

3. Ibid.

Chapter 16
Survey Results: "Why Did I Leave Work or Reduce My Work Hours?"

1. Kristen Davis, "Can You Afford to Quit Work?" *Parents*, April 2005, 105.

2. George Hagen, "9 Things You Should Know About Stay-at-Home Dads," *Parents*, February 2004, 137.

Chapter 17
From a Child's Perspective

1. Dreskin and Dreskin, *The Day Care Decision*, 49.

2. Ibid., 107.

3. Louise Continelli, "Profile: Debbie Buckley: Former Nurse Tells How She Chose to Put Family First Over Profession," *Buffalo News*, November 5, 2007, D7.

Chapter 18
"How Might My Occupation Change?"

1. Belkin, "The Opt-Out Revolution," 2.

Chapter 19
Quantity versus Quality

1. Smith, "Professional Women Embarking Upon Motherhood in their 30's—Perceptual Changes in Success and Goals," 92.
2. Dreskin and Dreskin, *The Day Care Decision*, 115.
3. Galinsky, *Ask the Children*, 72.

Chapter 21
Who Takes Care of the Children?

1. Galinsky, *Ask the Children*, 153.

Chapter 22
What Will You Encounter When You Want to *Increase* Your Work Hours?

1. Workforce Week e-newsletter, May 28–June 3, 2006, vol. 7, issue 22. An article based on the Workforce Week e-newsletter was in the BNHRA (Buffalo Niagara Human Resources Association) August 2006 newsletter *Network*.
2. Michelle Kearns, "Business Today," *The Buffalo News*, July 9, 2006, C1–C2.
3. Ibid.
4. Ibid.

Chapter 24
Final Advice and Thoughts

1. Taken from *Walking the Talk Together*, by Eric Harvey and Alexander Lucia, and adapted from *The Star Thrower*, by Loren Eisley.

About the Author

In order to balance time with family more effectively, Cathi Brese Doebler left her full-time job as a Manager of Performance Development and started her own consulting business. The main reason for this change was that Ms. Doebler wanted to be the main caretaker for her children. She was able to balance time with her children while running her own part-time consulting business.

Nine years after going to part-time hours, she has shared her insight into the struggle parents face when making a transition from being full-time employees to part-time employees or stay-at-home parents.

Ms. Doebler is a mother of two, and has experience in writing, recruiting, management coaching, and training. Ms. Doebler has a Master of Science in Corporate Communication from Ithaca College and 15 years of experience in the Human Resources field. Her current consulting work is in Performance Consulting, Meeting Facilitation, Training, and Writing.

Ms. Doebler resides in New York State with her family. This is her first book.

Some quotes from Ms. Doebler's clients include:

> "Why do I continue to work with Cathi? Because she's smart, a fast learner, understands instructional design and its value to the organization. What caused me to first be impressed with her is her relentless persistence at delivering great quality. She doesn't stop until the job is not just perfect, but done beyond expectations. I continue to hire her at every opportunity because she does great work and makes me look like a hero. Oh, and she's a heck of a lot of fun to work with!"
>
> –Jonathan Vehar, Senior Partner, New & Improved, LLC

> "While some individuals can offer a spark or two of insight and inspiration to a situation, Cathi is an entire meteor shower. For this office she has been a wellspring of ideas, creativity and solutions, which she is so ready and forth coming with, that you know experience has been her greatest teacher. Her experiences have been my resource without measure."
>
> –Hal Boltz, Quality Assurance, Erie County Department of Social Services

> Cathi Doebler possesses the knowledge and the interpersonal skills that enabled my staff to apply performance consulting theory to their own everyday work. She is professional, organized and always prepared. What a joy to work with!
>
> –Judith Holthoff, Director of HRD/QAT,
> Erie County Department of Social Services

Helping parents give more time,
love and balance for their families…

SPEAKING ENGAGEMENTS

Cathi Brese Doebler is a motivated organizer teaching family-oriented financial responsibility and decision making. Through integrity and faith-based principles, Cathi brings practical know-how and enthusiasm for flourishing families to her presentations.

Bringing 15 years of business coaching and training experience, her sessions are realistic, focusing on tools and ideas for families searching for balance in how they spend their time.

For information on speaking engagements, visit: **www.ditchthe.com**